Wolfgang Fallmann

CRYPTO INVESTOR MINDSET

Principles for avoiding mistakes in
thinking when investing in Bitcoin
and cryptocurrencies

1st edition 2020

Copyright © 2020 DI Wolfgang Fallmann, MSc

ISBN: 978-3-9519854-3-5

This book is also available as an e-book.
www.btc-machine.com

Table of Contents

Foreword

The peak of my investments in cryptocurrencies was reached when my portfolio had reached over 650% in profit. I was on the phone with my best friend at the time to report how well my investments had performed. He told me that I should realize a part of the profits. My ego, greed, overestimation of myself, the endowment effect and other factors led to the fact that I did not realize the profits and lost everything again. In the past, I had made mistakes in investing, but never analyzed them. I simply ignored them, blamed the market or others for my failure and simply forgot about the bad investment. Next time I will do better, I thought. It took many more failures until I finally realized that I was making the same mistakes over and over again, that it was up to me and not other people, the news, the experts or the market. When the pain of the constant losses reached a maximum this time, I started to deal intensively with myself, my thoughts, emotions and human errors of thought. That was the turning point.

A large part of traders and investors are losing money on the markets. People believe that they can make rational and good decisions. Unfortunately, this is not true for the majority of people and for most investment decisions. All too often we allow ourselves to be fooled into relying too much on our current mood, feelings and emotions when making decisions. We believe our first intuitive answer, but it usually causes mistakes. We tend to be risk takers when we lose and risk averse when we win. We tend to overestimate our knowledge of the world and underestimate the role that chance plays in events. Because our brain is not designed for this, we ignore statistical facts and overweight unlikely events. The weightings for our decisions do not match the associated probabilities and we systematically deviate from the expected value, which is costly. When making financial decisions, we attach much more value to profits and losses than to the asset situation itself. These and other factors cause predictable errors in thinking. These errors lead to bad decisions and this in turn leads to losses in our investments.

Daniel Kahneman, an Israeli-American psychologist and economist, and his colleague Amos Tversky spent decades researching how people make decisions under uncertainty. They developed the new theory of expectations, which is the basis of behavioral economics. Kahneman received the Nobel Prize in 2002 for his work "Psychology of judgement and decision-making". Amos Tversky (who unfortunately died in 1996), Kahneman, and other colleagues (such as the behavioral economist and psychologist Dan Ariely) influenced me and therefore this book with their research and experiments on human decision behavior.

A further influence is the financial mathematician, risk and chance researcher Nassim Nicholas Taleb. He is an unconventional thinker, provocative researcher and bestselling author, who also influenced me and this book with his insights from his twenty years of working as a securities and options trader. Taleb focuses his investments primarily on unexpected, sudden market events (so-called black swans) that cause massive market movements and drive many investors to ruin because they do not expect such market anomalies.

The US-American entrepreneur and founder Ray Dalio had a further influence. Dalio built up "Bridgewater Associates", a globally known and highly successful hedge fund. Dalio attributed his success to two things. First, he modeled complicated markets as a simple machine. He examines how the individual parts work together, trying to understand how markets work. The market is made up of human actors, all of whom are subject to the same psychological effects and errors of reasoning. Understanding human behavior in investment decisions is therefore part of this machine. Secondly, it establishes generally valid rules, so-called principles, which it applies, refines and develops again and again. These principles are the secret of the extraordinary success of his fund and his company.

At the end of this book, I derive generally applicable principles for investing in Bitcoin and cryptocurrencies from the research on human behavior in decisions by Kahneman, Tversky, Ariely and other colleagues, Taleb's insights into the risk and behavior of market participants when investing, and Dalio's principles of success. You should apply these principles, adapt them to your personal needs and develop them further. These principles are the foundation for successful trading and investing in Bitcoin and cryptocurrencies. The goal of this book is to show you the unconscious errors of reasoning so that you can learn from them and thus improve your judgements and decisions when making investments. This requires a certain discipline and effort on your part. Admitting to yourself that you are making errors in judgment is the first and most important step. An open mind set and the willingness to exchange old beliefs for new ones is a basic requirement. To get the most out of this book, you should have a pen and a notepad ready. There are some examples and thought experiments that you should definitely try out. They are shown in *italics*. On the one hand, you will see that you yourself are prone to errors in thinking and, on the other hand, it will help you to avoid such errors in the future, since you have thought through these examples and noted down the result. Some things may not be intuitively understandable at first and it takes time to understand them correctly and to put them into practice. Therefore, consider this book as your coach and companion, reference it from time to time and learn the principles for successful investing. You will almost certainly be surprised at some points and may doubt the truth. Our brain likes to deceive us, and it will not make it easy for you to see this. I therefore recommend that you additionally read the books "Fast Thinking, Slow Thinking" by Daniel Kahneman, "Black Swan" and "Fools of Chance" by Taleb and "Principles" by Ray Dalio. They will provide you with added value not only when investing, but also in other areas of life.

I knew subconsciously that my trading and investment results depended largely on my decisions in the markets. I felt that sometimes I would have had to behave differently in order to make better investment decisions and yet I always made the same mistakes. Fortunately, I came to a point where I questioned my actions. This book is the result of this long journey. I assure you that if you understand and apply the contents of this book, it will open your eyes as much as it did mine. Your investments and trades will improve, and it will also bring you added value in other areas of your life.

Get something to write with now and get started!

Introduction: How we think and make decisions

In the 1970s, two assumptions about human behavior were considered proven. First, people generally behave rationally, and they usually think clearly. Second, emotions such as fear, hatred, affection, etc. explain most cases where people deviate from rationality. Daniel Kahneman and Amos Tversky refuted this. In their new Prospect Theory, they analyzed decision making under uncertainty and concluded that people behave much more irrationally than expected.

The two systems

People have two systems with which they think:

> System I: The fast, intuitive thinking
> System II: The slow, cognitive thinking

System I is responsible for our fully automated perception processes and automated routines. It takes control in emergency situations to protect us and assigns top priority to actions that serve self-protection. It is always active; it cannot be turned off and that is the reason why mistakes happen to us that System II does not notice. Thinking happens automatically and unconsciously. It is stereotyping and emotional. System I works almost effortlessly. It is more influential than we subjectively feel and secretly controls many decisions. The reason why it is so difficult for us to think statistically is that System I is not designed for it.

System II is responsible for our slow thinking. It is the strenuous form of thinking. It is rarely active and we have to activate it, which takes effort. By activating System II, we act deliberately. It is tedious, it requires work and concentration. When System II is activated, our pupils dilate and the heartbeat increases. It requires attention and is disturbed when attention is withdrawn. System II is lazy and requires a minimum of work. It is logical, calculating and conscious. You can activate your System II by answering the following question:

How much is 17x24? Write down your answer.

There are often conflicts between the two systems. System II is responsible for self-control and processes the impulses of System I. System II controls System I. This control is important because System I can lead to massive misjudgments. However, this control is exhausting and takes energy. So, to increase the quality of our decisions, we should activate our System II and think "slower". However, System II is also not immune to misconceptions, as you will see below.

Test your systems using the following example:

One club and one ball costs $1.10. The club costs one dollar more than the ball. How much does the ball cost?
Write down your answer.

This example is known as the "bat-ball problem". Over 50 percent of students at the elite universities of Harvard, Princeton and MIT (Massachusetts Institute of Technology) gave the intuitive, wrong answer. At other universities, over 80 percent gave the wrong answer. If your answer was 10 cents, then you relied on the intuitive, fast System I and gave the wrong answer.

Now activate your System II and look at the example again and find out what the right answer is.

Write down your answer.

The solution to the problem is as follows: The club should cost 1 dollar "more than the ball". The two conditions, total cost equals $1.10 and club is $1 more expensive, are only met if the ball costs 5 cents and the club costs $1.05. This example shows that very many people trust their intuition (intuitive, fast System I) too much and do not question it (activation of System II).

Intellectual abbreviations

Performing several things at once (multitasking) is only possible if they are simple and undemanding, such as driving a car and talking to the passenger. A vivid example of this statement is the "Monkey Business Illusion".

Visit YouTube, search for "The Monkey Business Illusion" by Daniel Simons and watch the video before you read on.

This video reveals two facts about mental processes. First, we can be blind to the obvious and second, we are also blind to our blindness. When we focus our attention on something, we often overlook other unexpected things. This means that when System II is active, we are blind to other things. So, in our thinking we are subject to an illusion. We are deceived by ourselves.

Our brain is lazy and looks for mental shortcuts to reach a decision quickly. In psychology this is somewhat unwieldly called heuristics (or judgment heuristics). In other words, heuristics are simple rules for quick assessment or decision making. In many life situations it is rarely possible or often too time-consuming to research countless alternatives, estimate probabilities and then weigh them up rationally. People often like to disregard statistical facts and prefer to rely on simplifying heuristics to make a difficult judgement. This reliance on heuristics causes predictable errors (also called bias) in our predictions. Especially when investing, we encounter these errors all too often and do not even notice them. Among the best-known judgment heuristics are the

- Affect heuristics
- Availability heuristic
- Representativeness heuristics
- Anchoring heuristics

We will discuss these and other heuristics in detail throughout the book.

CHAPTER 1: Why we should not believe ourselves

The WYSIATI rule: Only what you know counts

WYSIATI stands for "What you see is all there is". Daniel Kahneman found that our brain only processes the information currently available and that we make our intuitive, hasty conclusions based on this limited database. Our intuitive, fast-thinking system in our brain is to blame. Daniel Kahneman calls this System I. It makes us insensitive to the quality and quantity of information. The presentation of one-sided information (only one side of a story) has a strong effect on our human judgment. Test subjects were given one-sided information and they were also told that it was one-sided information. Although the test subjects were given the opportunity to get a picture of the other situation (activation of System II), they did not do so. It is also interesting that people who only have one-sided information are much more confident in their judgement than people who have a picture of both sides. The consistency of the information from which we construct a story is more important to us than the completeness of that information. The strength of our inner conviction of a matter, therefore, depends on the context (coherence) of the story we construct from the available information. If we know little, it is easier to put together this little information into a consistent story than if we know a lot. This is why WYSIATI also makes sure that we do not take more information or we might spoil our story.

Regarding our investments, this means that we only get as much information as we need for a coherent story, that can be logically explained to us. We also feel secure in our judgment. We do not make it our business to look at the other side of a story as well, as this could potentially spoil our story and make us more uncertain about our predictions. In short, we often make investment decisions based only on the information currently available. We do not think about the things we do not know.

Hindsight bias: Why we knew it all the time

I remember back to the big Bitcoin hype in November 2017, when the mood in the Bitcoin and Altcoin market was positive. One of my friends invested in Bitcoin at that time. He was convinced that the Bitcoin price would rise far above $20,000 and could also give plausible reasons for this. Half a year later, (the Bitcoin price collapsed and was about $8000) I met him again and we talked about his investment. He said that he knew that the Bitcoin price would never rise above $20,000 and he gave me plausible reasons for this again. He did not notice it himself, but I could still remember the situation at the time, how he told me with conviction and enthusiasm about the reasons why the Bitcoin price would go up so high. But when he later remembered back, he knew nothing more about it and even said the opposite of what he said at the time. He was subject to the so-called back-shooting error.

The hindsight bias, also known as the "I knew it all along" effect, is the tendency of people to believe in retrospect that they knew something they did not know. This means that when we know the result and remember it, we are reproducing a distortion of the real result. The regression error is a cognitive illusion. The human mind has a deficient ability to reconstruct past states of knowledge or beliefs that have changed. Once you have a new view of things, you lose the ability to remember what you believed before you changed your mind.

Many psychologists have studied hindsight bias to find out what happens when we change our mind. When an event actually happened, respondents overestimated the probability they had previously attributed to the event ("I knew it all along"). If an event did not occur, they incorrectly remembered that they had always considered it unlikely. Further experiments showed that people not only predicted the accuracy of their own earlier ones, but also overestimated the accuracy of others. The backscatter error was also found in Wikipedia articles. It was found, for example, that in the case of catastrophes, the later versions of articles suggested more strongly that the catastrophe should have occurred.

The hindsight bias is a very strong effect. It also occurs when we know about the hindsight bias. We erroneously remember wrong facts when we remember our trades or investments at a later date. We overestimate the probability when an event really occurs ("I knew all along that the price was rising/falling") and we underestimate when an event has not occurred. For example, in retrospect we think that we have always correctly predicted the price, but this is usually not true. We only remember it wrong.

The outcome bias: In the end we always know everything better

My acquaintance made a loss when he invested in the hype back then. He bought in at a Bitcoin price of about $14,000 and held his positions long after the price had collapsed after the hype. When we talked about this investment, he said it was a bad investment. But that was not quite true, because after he bought in, the price went up to almost $20,000. Unfortunately, he missed the exit in time. By judging whether it was a good or bad decision, he committed the so-called "outcome bias".

Outcome bias is the tendency of people to judge a decision by its final outcome rather than by the quality of the decision at the time of the decision. So, we judge our trades and investments at the end when we have realized a loss or a profit. This is an outcome bias, because we actually have to judge whether the decision at the beginning of the trade or investment was good or not. Not every loss trade was a bad decision and not every profit trade was a good decision. In the evaluation, the hindsight bias exerts a damaging influence. It causes one to judge a decision by its outcome (for example, positive or negative outcome of an investment) rather than judging whether the decision-making process was good. If the results are bad, investors think that the decision was bad, and they did not see the signs. However, they forget that these signs only became visible afterwards. Some investments that sounded reasonable in advance may appear negligent in retrospect. The worse the consequences, the greater the hindsight bias. Conversely, investors who were lucky are rewarded and not punished for taking disproportionately high risks. Instead, it is believed that these investors had the intuition and foresight to predict success. In retrospect, those who doubted these investors are then judged to be cautious and weak. Some fortunate ventures can then surround a ruthless investor with a halo of foresight and boldness (see later Halo Effect).

Investors often believe they have understood the past and that the future can be predicted and controlled. Unfortunately, this is often an illusion. These illusions are reassuring, they reduce our fear if we are aware of the uncertainty of the future. We all strive for the reassuring message that our actions have the desired consequences, and that wisdom and courage are crowned with success. Test yourself:

Write down today's rate of the cryptocurrencies in which you want to invest or have already invested. Now make an estimate of where the exchange rate of all cryptocurrencies will be in exactly 6 months. Also, document why you believe that the exchange rate will be exactly there. What information or factors have you used for your estimate? Document as precisely as possible! Put a reminder in your calendar and check the reality with your forecast in 6 months.

This task leads to the painful insight that we are almost always wrong with our predictions - although in retrospect we like to claim the opposite (hindsight bias). The only way to avoid the outcome bias is to keep a diary of our trading and investment decisions and to document everything that led us to this decision. After some trades and investments, we can evaluate which original decisions led to which result and adjust our strategy accordingly without committing the outcome bias. We can learn from past trading decisions and derive action principles for future decisions.

Confirmation bias: Why we lose money when we meet our own expectations

Confirmation bias is the tendency of people to seek, select and interpret information in such a way that their own expectations are met (confirmed). This has far-reaching implications for investors, as they specifically look for information that supports their basic assumption (for example, that the share price must move up/down). In addition, data is selected that supports their conviction and the rest of the data is ignored because it is not supportive. In addition, investors tend to interpret ambiguous evidence as support for their existing position. The effect is strongest with desired outcomes, emotionally charged issues and deep-rooted beliefs.

Peter Wason was the first to develop a theory on this bias in the 1960s. A series of psychological experiments indicated that people are biased to confirm their existing beliefs. Later work interpreted these results as a tendency to test ideas one-sidedly, to focus on only one possibility and to ignore alternatives (myside bias, is an alternative name for the confirmation error). In certain situations, this tendency can influence people's conclusions. Explanations for the error are wishful thinking and the limited human ability to process information. Another explanation is that people show the confirmation error because they weigh the cost of injustice rather than investigating in a neutral, scientific way. Scientists and intelligent people can also be prone to confirmation bias.

Confirmation bias contributes to excessive confidence in personal beliefs and can maintain or even strengthen those beliefs in the face of evidence to the contrary. These prejudices have led to poor decisions being made in political, organizational, financial and scientific contexts. For example, a bias in confirmation leads to systematic errors in scientific research based on inductive reasoning (the gradual accumulation of supporting evidence). For example, a police officer with prejudice will tend to look for confirmation of a suspect at the beginning of an investigation rather than focus on rebutting evidence. Confirmation bias can cause investors to be overconfident and ignore evidence that their strategies are losing money. In studies of stock markets, investors made more profit by resisting the confirmation bias.

What can investors do about the audit error? We encounter the confirmation bias at the:
- Pre-assumption or basic attitude before the search for information
- Search for information
- Information selection
- Interpretation of the information

Traders and investors have strong presumptions or basic attitudes to an investment before searching for information. It is important to deal intensively with one's own pre-assumptions and to make them self-conscious. Through reflection processes and critical, open discussions, e.g., with a mentor or an investor who disagrees, one's own basic assumptions and prejudices can be identified. Take the opposite view "for reasons of argumentation". Avoid a distorted search for information. Consciously search for information that can potentially refute your own assumptions.

Consciously search for exceptions. Search consciously for other representations, visit other websites than normal, search for new groups in which you exchange information. Look for facts (not opinions!) and take the time to check them. When interpreting the information, carry out a critical analysis of your own conclusions. Look for alternative explanations. Question situations (e.g., "Is cryptocurrency X really a project with future prospects?"). You should regularly and consciously question your assumptions and be prepared to reject assumptions and accept views that contradict your opinion. See things as they really are and not as you would like them to be. In this way, you can increase the chances that situations will be assessed as objectively as possible. In a thought experiment, imagine that your investments have collapsed and ask yourself why this might happen (see Chapter 7: Pre-Mortem Method). In order to check opposite statements, use the hypothesis test method (see Chapter 7: Hypothesis Test Method).

Clustering illusion: Why we see things that do not exist

Like many other investors who enter trading, I stumbled over chart patterns and chart formations at the beginning. I devoured countless books on technical analysis and chart patterns and was captivated by the myriad possibilities that were available. Gaps, spikes, trend lines, trend channels, double high, double low, triple high, triple low, cup and inverted cup, shoulder-head-shoulder, inverted shoulder-head-shoulder, rising/sinking/symmetric triangles or wedges, flags and pennants, candlestick patterns, etc. I was sure to find the holy grail in it and programmed countless automated trading systems for the currency market based on chart patterns and indicators. I tested countless systems with a wide range of parameters, performed back and forward tests and logged long-term performance. What did I learn after three years of hard work? The performance of trading systems based on chart patterns and (mainly price-based) technical indicators is no better than a coin flip. One reason for this can be found in the clustering illusion.

The clustering illusion is that humans are programmed to recognize patterns. In sufficiently large (random) amounts of data, random patterns inevitably emerge. We have the tendency to recognize patterns where there are none at all and attribute a meaning to them. We also tend not to recognize random events as such.

Consider the following three sequences of a coin toss. K stands for the "head side" and Z for the "tails side" of a coin.
  1. *ZKZKZZ*
  2. *KKKZZZZ*
  3. *ZZZZZZ*
Are all three consequences equally likely? Write down your answer!

You can convince yourself of randomly occurring (but not random-looking) sequences of letters if you simply pick up a coin, toss it a few times and write down the results. During my experiment, the following sequence of letters was created:

KKKZZKKZZZZZZZKZKZKZZKKKZKZKKKKZZZKKZZZ
ZZZZZZZKZKZZ

Remarkable are the many successive Z's at the end of the sequence of letters. It seems as if this was not accidental. The three sequences from the above example are also taken from this series. Here for illustration in brackets:

KKKZZKKZZZZZZ(ZKZKZKZZ)KKKZKZK(KKKZZZ)KKZ
ZZZ(ZZZZZZ)KZKZZ

So, you can see that the rows of letters in the example were created purely by chance, although they do not look random.

Try it yourself and get a feeling for what random can look like. Take a coin and toss it a few times and write down the letter sequence!

The clustering illusion also appeared at impact sites of airplane bombs in London during World War II. It was thought that the drop points were planned and that there was a pattern. However, calculations showed that they were simply, randomly distributed. A typical clustering illusion is also when people recognize faces or figures in the clouds in the sky. Do they remember the "Mars face" or divine figures on burnt toast? All illusions. The clustering illusion also occurs when we look at stock or cryptocurrency prices. Everywhere we look we find some pattern in the charts and assign meaning to these patterns. Especially in technical analysis, the clustering illusion plays an important role and can lead us astray. In addition, different people see different patterns in the same charts and ascribe different meanings to them. The clustering illusion arises, among other things, due to the human representativeness heuristic (see chapter 6) and confirmation bias.

See for yourself how different investors discover patterns in price charts and interpret them. Visit the tradingview.com page and have a look at the "Ideas" section. What conclusion do you draw from this? Write down your answer!

The sunk cost effect: Why we stick to investments when it no longer makes sense

I invested not only in Bitcoin, but also in several Altcoins. To be precise, there were over 60 different ones. The Altcoin market was booming thanks to the massive increase in Bitcoin. Every day, new Altcoins came onto the market, suggesting that they were the ideal cryptocurrency for this or that problem. After the hype when Bitcoin and Altcoins massively collapsed, I again invested money in a few of my beloved Altcoin projects. "Buying cheap" was the credo and was propagated by many media, Youtubers and by the projects themselves. The majority of the projects are worth nothing today. Only later did I realize that I was subject to the sunk cost effect.

The sunk-cost-effect is the tendency to stick to a project for a longer period of time, if an investment in the form of time, effort or money has already been made. The decision to invest additional financial resources in a loss-making business when better investment opportunities are available is called the "sunk cost fallacy". Sunk costs are costs that have already been incurred and can no longer be reversed (e.g., through sale). Since people do not always follow rationality, irreversible costs are often considered in retrospect. From a rational point of view, this is unjustified and distorts the economically optimal decision process. A rational thinking person recognizes the sunk cost effect and acts accordingly.

The sunk cost effect is a costly mistake that causes people to hold on too long to unloved jobs, to stay in unhappy relationships or marriages, or to get stuck on hopeless projects. The effect occurs, for example, when products are launched onto the market. Product launches often have high costs. If the product should not be purchased, then the costs already incurred for the product launch should not be taken into account for the further decision to leave the product on the market or take it off the market. Only the future chances of the product on the market count. Frequently sunk costs occur also, if with a planning of projects, the real costs exceed the planning. Therefore, future decisions should not be influenced by these original (sunk) costs. Investors often base their sales decisions on the price they paid at the time of purchase. However, the price at which one entered the market in the past is irrelevant for assessing the future development of an investment. You may know the saying: "You can't throw good money after bad". This rule is based on the sunk cost effect and thus expresses that you should not throw more money to recoup losses just because you have already invested money. However, we let ourselves be influenced by it because we have already invested so much.

The endowment effect: Why something becomes more expensive when we own it

A further phenomenon I observed with myself and also with other crypto investors is that we could not separate very comfortably from our beloved cryptocurrencies, although they had already massively fallen in value and future prospects did not look so rosy. We were subject to the endowment effect.

The endowment effect was first mentioned by Richard Thaler, an economist at the University of Chicago, around 1980. He was already conducting studies on irrational human behavior in the early 1970s. Studies have shown that the value of a good increases for people when they own it. This means that a person's willingness to buy and sell for one and the same good differs and thus reflects irrational behavior. This is called the endowment effect. In an experiment by Kahneman, Knetsch and Thaler in the early 1990s with coffee cups, half of the participants in the experiment each received a cup as a gift and were asked at what price they would sell. The other half were asked at what price they would buy the cups. The average price of the "selling group" was $7.12, while the price of the "buying group" was $2.87.

The explanation of the endowment effect lies in the prospect theory (we will discuss the prospect theory in a later chapter):

When we own something (that in some way provides us with value), we have a certain "unwillingness" feeling associated with giving that good away. If we do not possess something, then we have a "pleasure-feeling" connected with the acquisition of the good. Because of loss aversion (see Chapter 4), these two feelings are weighted differently. Giving something away generates more (on average about twice as much) listlessness than the acquisition generates desire. The emotion of loss is stronger than the emotion of gain. People who act rationally have no endowment effect because the asymmetry between the good feeling of getting something and the bad feeling of giving something away is irrelevant. The effect does not occur in routine trading transactions, such as exchanging one five dollar note for five one-dollar notes. Even if you buy something, the loss aversion is irrelevant. You do not feel a loss when you exchange money for something. The endowment effect is not relevant for goods that are intended for exchange, it only affects goods that have a practical value.

The endowment effect can also occur with Bitcoin and other cryptocurrencies. We see a certain value in a cryptocurrency and have an "unpleasant feeling" associated with giving it away. The market value of self-held cryptocurrencies for the owner is above the purchase price. With a sales decision, thus always this purchase price is considered. The endowment effect can lead now to the fact that the realizable selling price is estimated as unacceptably low and it does not come thereby to the sales. The price of a cryptocurrency depends on the expectations of the market participants regarding the future development of the price. It can happen now that we do not evaluate rationally with the evaluation of the price of cryptocurrencies but follow other motives. This happens above all if the cryptocurrency concerned is in the possession of the owner. The one who owns the cryptocurrency itself will therefore overvalue the cryptocurrencies. The endowment effect occurs especially with inexperienced traders. The so-called "Hodlers" have a strong endowment effect. They hold on to the purchased cryptocurrency, because they are of the opinion that it will rise in value and do not want to sell, therefore, too favorably. The question, which one must ask oneself, is: How long do you want to hold the cryptocurrency? Experienced traders are subject to less influence. The experienced dealers ask themselves, how much do they want to possess this property compared with other things, which they could have instead.

Optimism bias: Why our optimism costs us money

The 2017 crypto hype was mainly driven by retail investors. I can still remember a friend calling me and asking what Bitcoin was and how to buy it. There were many people at that time who invested in Bitcoin and other cryptocurrencies, even though they had not yet encountered them, let alone knew what they were or how they worked. They were all driven by the positive mood in the market and the possible profit prospects. However, many were subject to the distortion of optimism.

The optimism bias is a cognitive bias that makes people believe that they are more likely to experience a positive event themselves. It is also known as unrealistic optimism or comparative optimism.

Optimism is widespread and goes beyond gender, ethnicity, nationality and age. The optimism bias has even been observed in animals such as rats and birds. It works intuitively and subconsciously in most people, so they do not notice it themselves unless they are self-confessed optimists.

There are four factors that cause a person to be optimistically biased: their desired final state, their cognitive mechanisms, the information they have about themselves compared to others, and their general mood. The optimistic tendency can be seen in a number of situations. For example:

- People who are more optimistic about their own future than it actually is
- People who consider their partner's divorce or professional failure to be less serious
- People who believe that they live healthier and longer than they actually do
- People who believe that they are less likely to be victims of crime
- Smokers who believe that they are less likely to develop lung cancer or disease than other smokers
- First-time bungee jumpers who believe they are less at risk for injury than other jumpers
- Traders who believe they are less exposed to potential losses in the markets or
- Investors who take too high risks in the markets (e.g., buy single risky stocks instead of an index)

Although the tendency to be optimistic occurs both in positive events (e.g., when you think you are financially more successful than others) and in negative events (e.g., when you are less likely to have a drinking problem), there is more research and evidence that the tendency for negative events is stronger (valence effect).

The consequences of these two types of events are different: positive events often lead to well-being and self-esteem, while negative events lead to consequences that are associated with a higher risk, such as risky behavior and the taking of no preventive safety measures.

The valence effect has been studied by Ron S. Gold and his team since 2003. They formulated questions for the same event in different ways: Some participants received information about the conditions that promote a particular health-related event, such as the development of heart disease, and were asked to evaluate the comparative likelihood that they would experience the event. Other participants received consistent information about the conditions that prevent the same event and were asked to evaluate the comparative likelihood that they would avoid the event. They found that unrealistic optimism was greater for negative valence than for positive. Valence effects, which are also considered a form of cognitive distortion, have several real effects. For example, it can cause investors to overestimate the future profits of a company and this could contribute to the company tending to become overpriced. In terms of achieving organizational goals, this could encourage people to create unrealistic schedules, which could contribute to a so-called planning fallacy (also called planning miscalculation, see next chapter), which often leads to bad decisions and project abandonment.

The optimism bias is the basis for overestimating oneself (see chapter 3) and this in turn is the basis for ignorance of risks. This increases the probability of failure of a project, a company or an investment.

Research has shown that it is very difficult to remove the optimism bias. One way, is to consider how the average of other people in a situation score. Ideally, there is statistical data to rely on (see Chapter 6, Base rate fallacy). If you are very far from the average, you either need good reasons for the deviation or you are simply too optimistic.

Another possibility is to compare the probability of an event occurring to yourself with the probability of family members or close friends. In addition, the actual experience of an event leads to a decrease in the optimistic tendency. While this is only true for events with previous experience, knowing the unknown leads to less optimism.

The planning fallacy: We always need longer than we think

When we set up the Altcoin mining plant in 2017, there were delays in commissioning. Reasons included overly optimistic estimates for the construction of the mining rigs, different environmental conditions and unexpected events (such as rain). A rig consisted of six graphics cards, a mainboard with CPU and RAM, a power supply and lots of cables. We had to assemble over 170 of them. For the estimation of the total duration, we stopped the assembly of a rig in our office and calculated the time plus an extra charge for the 170 rigs. But we did not think about the possible adverse circumstances that would happen to us during the real setup. The rigs were set up in two twenty-foot sea containers standing on supports, which were connected to a hydroelectric power plant and were placed in front of the power plant in a parking lot. One factor that we had not considered during the planning was the ascent and descent into the containers. At first this sounds banal, but if you have to climb in and out of the containers countless times a day via a short ladder, it takes time. Another factor was that the space in the container was very tight and this took additional time during assembly. Another consideration was the weather. Fortunately, we often had nice weather, which was good for the atmosphere during the assembly. However, we also had rain, and this led to delays. All in all, we had reasonable time planning and yet we needed longer.

The planning fallacy is the tendency of people and companies to underestimate the time it takes to complete a task or project. The most prominent example of a planning fallacy is the construction of the Berlin-Brandenburg Airport (BER). The first planning took place in 1995, when the calculated costs for the first stage of expansion amounted to over 1.1 million D-Mark. Adjusted for inflation, this would have been approximately 800 million euros. Construction started in September 2006 and the first commissioning was planned for

November 2011. This date and many other opening dates were not met. The many delays were caused by poor construction planning, which resulted in the responsible supervisory authorities not approving the construction, lack of building supervision, incorrect planning and exploding costs. After all deficiencies had been remedied, the airport was finally put into operation at the end of April 2020. The estimated total costs finally amounted to 7.3 billion euros.

The English term for the planning fallacy was suggested by Daniel Kahneman and Amos Tversky in 1979. The interesting thing about this effect is that it only affects their own predictions about the duration of a project. When outside third parties estimate the time required for the duration of a project, they show a more pessimistic tendency and overestimate the time needed to complete it. After further research, Lovallo and Kahneman proposed an extended definition of the term in 2003. It became apparent that not only time but also costs are underestimated. Thus, according to the new definition, the planning fallacy leads not only to exceeding the planned time period but also to a cost explosion and a lower benefit than previously planned.

Also, when investing, the planning mistakes will possibly come to you. For example, if you invest in crypto projects, you are taking into account the fact that there will be a planning fallacy and that schedules and costs for a project or product development will not be met as originally planned. If you are developing your own trading or investment system, you are likely to underestimate the time it takes to develop a profitable system.

Daniel Kahneman, Amos Tversky and Bent Flyvbjerg developed what is known as "Reference Class Forecasting" to eliminate or at least reduce the effects of optimism bias (and thus planning fallacy) when making decisions. The forecast is based on the results of similar situations in the past.

Therefore, it is important to document projects sufficiently in order to be able to fall back on them later. Put yourself in the position of a third party and use the outside view. An outside perspective shifts the focus from the specific characteristics of the current situation, to the statistical characteristics of the results in similar situations and helps to reduce planning fallacies. Be rather pessimistic when planning. Use the ideomotor phenomenon (see Priming, Chapter 2) to influence your mood and thus optimism in planning.

CHAPTER 2: Why we should not trust our surroundings

Anchoring effect: How any number influences our investment decisions

When trading and investing in cryptocurrencies, we are constantly surrounded by news, media reports, YouTube videos, Twitter news, telegram chats and much more. On all these channels, we encounter a wide variety of numbers on current prices, support and resistance levels, all-time highs and lows, price prospects and other numbers. Subconsciously we are influenced by these and other numbers that have nothing to do with cryptocurrencies. This is known as the anchoring effect.

The anchoring effect, also known as anchor heuristics, is the fact that people are influenced in their number estimations by existing environmental information (especially numbers) without being aware of this influence. The consequence is that the result is shifted in the direction of the anchor. If we have to estimate an unknown quantity, we look for a certain value for this unknown quantity. In doing so, we orientate ourselves at numbers, which can be recalled quickly in our memory or at numbers, which we have seen or heard immediately before. Our estimates therefore remain close to this number. This means that every number presented as a solution to an estimation problem creates an anchoring effect. Experiments on the anchoring effect have shown that judgements made by people are influenced by numbers that obviously have no relevance to the question asked. The anchoring effect is so robust, because a subconscious "priming" takes place and we do not even notice that we are influenced by the number. Anchoring effects are so strong that even experts, who know about the effect, are subject to it. One way to weaken the anchoring effect is to become aware of the effect and ask yourself, what answer would you have given without the anchor. Ideally, one relies on data-based decisions. In price negotiations, it helps to put yourself in the position of the other party and consider which anchor he or she would set.

An example of the anchoring effect:

Was Mahatma Gandhi older or younger than 144 years when he died? How old was Mahatma Gandhi when he died? Write down the age at which you think Gandhi died.

This example illustrates the absurdity that anchoring effects can have. You must have been aware that Mahatma Gandhi was younger than 144 years. However, the estimate of the age of his death towards the anchor (144 years) was unconsciously influenced. If I had asked the same question without the anchor, the estimate would have tended to be a younger age. This experiment has been confirmed in countless tests. Other examples of anchoring effects are:

- Donor organizations often use an amount as an anchor. E.g., "Already 30 Euros help"
- When shopping: "Now reduced to 50%" it is suggested that one buys half as cheap as normal
- Speed limits on freeways
- The amount of the tip. E.g., in the USA 10 to 20 percent
- For salary negotiations
- When budgeting
- For purchase and sales talks: Depending on which side you are on, the anchoring effect will either act on you or you will act on someone else with the anchoring effect. In price negotiations, you can take advantage of the anchoring effect by quoting a price first.

Especially in money matters, the anchoring effect has a strong impact, such as on amounts we donate, on the cost of buying a home, on salary negotiations or the price of shares or cryptocurrencies. With Bitcoin there are some numbers, which occur generally readily in the news and media more frequently and thus in our brain's "anchor". In addition, count

- $20,000, because this is almost the all-time high of the

Bitcoin
- $10,000, because Bitcoin has already reached this value several times and the media like to use this figure when the price comes close
- $100,000 because some Bitcoin fans see the price there in the long term
- $1.000.000 because some Bitcoin enthusiasts see the price there
- $3000, was the last low after the hype in 2018
- $7000, because many people believe that the exchange rate will not fall below this mark at present
- Etc.

When making investment decisions, we are therefore subject to precisely these anchors and our estimates are subconsciously influenced by them. For example, when estimating the price target, always remember that you have been influenced by the anchoring effect, for example by the media, friends or experts. People who are not aware of the anchoring effect will tend to place their positions at (or near) these anchors. For example, they will buy at $7000, set their Stop Loss at $6000 and their Take Profit at $10,000. We can use this to find out where liquidity is in the market. From the above example, we know that around $6000 and $10,000, there is concentrated selling liquidity. Due to the anchoring effect, higher liquidity can be expected in the market at very significant anchors (e.g., $10,000, $20,000, ...). Anchors that are currently not so prominent also accumulate liquidity, but less than the prominent anchors. Note that these anchors can change in value and significance over time. For example, it is possible that the $7000 becomes a significant anchor because the price forms a support or resistance zone on the chart. Gandhi was 79 years old when he died.

Priming: How our environment unconsciously influences us

In our decisions, we are not only influenced by numbers, but also by words, images, smells or gestures. The media and especially advertisers know about how these affect us and use them to "manipulate" us.

Priming is the tendency for a stimulus, such as a word, picture, smell, gesture or something similar, to unconsciously activate memory content and thus influence our decisions. Our actions and emotions are "primed" by events that we are not even aware of. Every day we are primed countless times and we also prime others without consciously noticing it.
An example of how we let ourselves be influenced by priming can be tried out by the following experiment.

Ask a friend, work colleague or family member the following questions and see what answer you get. The respondent should give the answer quickly and without thinking.
"What color is the snow?"
"What color is the wall?"
"What color are the clouds?"
"What does the cow drink?"

Typically, the answers are white, white, white and milk. However, an (adult) cow drinks water. This is a nice example of how we are subconsciously influenced by priming. Another well-known experiment on priming is that of Fritz Strack. In this experiment, they presented a questionnaire to a group of test subjects with the following questions: "How happy are you at the moment?" and "How many dates did you have in the past month?". There was no statistically significant correlation between the answers to these questions.
A second test group was presented with the same questionnaire, but with the questions "How many dates did you have in the past month?" and "How happy are you now?".

Interestingly, there was now a high correlation, as the respondents were primed and derived their state of happiness from the dates.

In priming experiments on money, it was found that people who were primed for "money" worked longer on difficult tasks before asking for help, were less helpful and preferred to be alone. Other tests have shown that subjects who have been primed on the topic of "aging" walk more slowly. Conversely, a test group was asked to move slowly like older people. It turned out that, in contrast to the control group, they found it much easier to remember words specific to their age. This situation became known as the "Florida effect". In another experiment, a group was primed for "success" by the words "win", "be successful" and "competition". The control group was presented with words like "turtle", "green" and "lamp". It was shown that the group primed for success achieved significantly better results in tasks. So, you can partly control your success in trading and investing by priming yourself on "success". If you tell yourself that you are a bad trader or investor, or that you are always unlucky, then you prime yourself on failure. Therefore, focus on your goals and solutions instead of obstacles and problems.

A special priming phenomenon is the ideomotor phenomenon (also called the carpenter effect). The ideomotor phenomenon influences an action by an imagination. This means that the seeing or thinking of a certain movement triggers the tendency to perform just this movement. A vivid example is a pendulum in the hand that magically changes from a circular movement to a rectilinear movement.

With the following exercise you can prime yourself:
Hold a pencil horizontally in your mouth between your teeth, so that the tip is pointing to one ear and the end to the other ear. This will force you to smile and make you happier or find things more fun. If you shape your mouth into an "O" and put the pencil in your mouth with the tip pointing

away from your face, you will be forced to frown and become more serious. Try it out!

You can take advantage of the ideomotor phenomenon when trading and investing. As we will see later, the quality of a decision depends on our mood. With the pencil we can primp ourselves into a different mood and thus influence the decision. For example, we are subject to overestimation of ourselves and distortion of optimism, which can lead to wrong decisions. With the ideomotor phenomenon, we can counteract an overly positive mood by forming the mouth into an "O", putting the pencil end into the mouth and we become more serious.

The mere-exposure-effect: The more the better

The mere-exposure-effect is the fact that people develop a more positive attitude towards images, videos or words that are shown more often. This effect was discovered by Robert Zajonc. Zajonc, who was born in Poland, was a U.S. psychologist and contributed significantly to the development of social psychology. In his experiment, he showed test subjects abstract forms and words in rapid succession. The test subjects rated the more frequently seen forms or words significantly more positively than the less frequently shown ones.

Examples of the effect:
- The more contact people have, the more likely they are to become friends
- If eggs from hens are exposed to a certain sound, this sound will later lead to reduced stress in the hatched chicks
- In marketing, this effect leads to a more positive perception of the company, products or services

through more frequently shown advertising

If, for example, many (positive) media reports about a cryptocurrency are shown, then we will build up a more positive attitude towards it through the mere-exposure effect than we would if there were no media reports. Thus, we are rather tempted to buy this cryptocurrency. Another example: The more media or experts write about the fact that the price will rise with the next Bitcoin Halving, the more investors will have a more positive attitude to this event and will invest, which will lead to a price increase.

Framing: Why we change our mind when the same thing is displayed differently

Framing is the tendency to draw different conclusions when the same information is presented differently. Different representations of the same information often evoke different emotions and influence our beliefs and preferences.

Example: What sounds more reassuring?
A: The probability of survival in the first month is 90 percent
B: The mortality rate is 10 percent in the first month
Write down your answer!

The two statements are equivalent. Statement A is nevertheless more reassuring than the equivalent statement B. Survival is good, dying is bad. The survival rate of 90 percent sounds better, while a death rate of 10 percent sounds terrible. However, people usually see only one formulation and only what you see counts (WYSIATI rule). Statement A is embedded in a "gain frame", i.e., the positive consequences of something is shown. Conversely, statement B is embedded in a loss frame, i.e., the negative consequences of a thing are shown. Usually, in health care measures the harmful consequences are usually pointed out, i.e., embedded in a loss frame. In prevention measures, however, messages embedded in a loss frame are more successful. A current example is the news about the coronavirus. It is always spoken of the people who have already died and not of those who have not died. It also makes a difference whether it is written about the mortality rate or survival rate. News and information influence how we process this information through their presentation and the way they are written.

Look at the result of the 2014 World Cup: Germany won. Argentina has lost. Both sentences describe the same end result. If one sentence is true, the other is also true. However, these two sentences do not have the same meaning in our memory and trigger different associations. The sentence "Germany has won" evokes thoughts about the German team and what they did to win (as long as we do not make a hindsight bias). The sentence "Argentina has lost" evokes thoughts of the Argentine team and of what they did to lose. This fact, that logically equivalent statements evoke different reactions, makes it difficult for people to always be rational.

Consider the following competition:

Would you enter a contest that has a 10 percent chance of winning $95 and a 90 percent chance of losing $5?
Write down your answer!

Would you pay $5 to enter a contest that has a 10 percent chance of winning $100 and a 90 percent chance of winning nothing?
Write down your answer!

Take a closer look at the two problems again and see for yourself that they are identical. In both problems there is the uncertain possibility of being $95 richer or relatively sure $5 poorer. People who make rational decisions would answer both questions the same. In reality, such people are rare, because answer two receives more positive answers than answer one. The difference is that in the first example the $5 is shown as a loss. In the second example the $5 is shown as a cost of a lottery. This means that a bad result is much more acceptable if it is represented as a cost of a raffle. It is less acceptable when it is described as losing a bet. We know this circumstance from the "loss aversion" (see later in the chapter prospect theory). Losses evoke stronger feelings than costs. Costs are not losses. This effect is often used in marketing. Consumers are more likely to forego a discount than to pay an extra charge. Both are economically equivalent, but emotionally equivalent they are not.

Consider the following example for framing Bitcoin:
1. The value of Bitcoin fell within only two weeks by 10 per cent.
2. Bitcoin is moving back towards its previous year's level, which was 10 percent lower than Bitcoin had this year.
3. The value of Bitcoin is currently falling, so far the losses amount to 10 per cent.
4. Bitcoin has suffered losses of only 10 percent despite the difficult market conditions.

The pure numerical value is always the same, the context however each time is different. With 1. we focus on a temporally very short-term crash of the value, with 2. we signal that Bitcoin probably cannot hold the high of this year, with 3. we imply a long lasting and persistent negative value development. In case 4. we perceive the losses as very small, in view of what could happen in the worst case. Bitcoin is perceived as "strong" here despite the losses that have occurred - even if this is not true at all.

If we are faced with a framing decision problem, we must activate our rotten system II and reformulate the specification (reframing). Reframing is an exhausting task and if there is no special reason, we accept problems as framed. A rational investor with a vigilant System II can learn this. In principle, use as little language as possible and focus on the numerical values. Also, the information should be reformulated in a profit frame. We will see things more positively if we frame the result according to how much money we kept instead of how much we lost. One example: I give you $50 on the condition that you have to play a game of chance. We now assume that you have lost $30. Now you can frame the result in two ways: You can either say that you have lost $30 or that you have been given $20.

Another way of reframing is to change the reference point. Here is an example: One of our investment positions is doing well and we are well into profit. Our brain automatically sets a new reference point from which the investment is evaluated. If the price changes and the profit decreases, we have the feeling of a loss. However, as long as the position is closed in profit, we should not feel a loss. In this case, we have to reframe by setting the reference point back to the original reference point when we entered.

CHAPTER 3: Why we should not believe experts and guides

The halo effect: Appearances are deceptive. Do not be dazzled!

Many crypto investors use YouTube to obtain information for their investment decisions. They follow people who regularly publish updates and investment tips on Bitcoin and other cryptocurrencies as video. When asked what enables these persons to publish qualitative and valid statements about the price development, I usually get the same answer: the number of followers. However, the number of followers has no statement about quality, only about entertainment value. If this were the case, documentary series would have to have much higher viewing figures than entertainment series. See for yourself by visiting an online newspaper and looking at which articles have the most comments. Guaranteed not on "important" topics, but on the "most entertaining" or "most interesting" ones. Especially investors who are new to the crypto world are subject to the halo effect and the illusion of competence (see next chapter).

The halo effect is a distortion in which one concludes from known characteristics of a person about unknown characteristics. Qualities such as attractiveness, disability or social status create a positive or negative impression. This impression "outshines" the perception of the person and the overall impression is disproportionately affected. For example, we will classify an attractive, sporty soccer player as above average and vice versa underestimate an ugly player (negative halo effect). The halo effect also occurs when a person is characterized by prominent, distinct characteristics or behavior. If we attach great importance to precisely these characteristics or behaviors, then the effect is particularly strong, and we therefore overestimate the effect particularly strongly.

Example: Foundation of Google
A year after the company was founded, the founders wanted

to sell Google for one million USD. But this was too expensive for the buyer. Fortunate circumstances led to Google's current result. This is intentionally a short and detailed narrative, because a more detailed story could give the feeling that we can learn useful lessons from the history of Google in general, which led the company to success. Unfortunately, there is much to suggest that the feeling of having learned something from Google's history is largely an illusion. The crucial test for the quality of an explanation is the question: "Can you predict the outcome in advance? You will agree that no story of Google's unlikely success will pass this test. No story can include the countless events that would have produced a different result. Our human brain does not deal with non-events. Many of Google's important decisions were based on decisions made by executives. It is precisely for this reason that we are tempted to overestimate the ability of skill and ability, and underestimate the share of happiness. Since it appears that every significant decision has been positive, this indicates flawless foresight. Had the decision-makers been a little unlucky in their decisions, it would have ruined each of the subsequent steps. The Halo effect adds the final touch to the whole story and gives the decision-makers an aura of invincibility. An experienced firefighter, who has had hundreds of assignments, has learned to "read" the fire and its effects and "foresee" possible dangers. He has learned to use his posture and his senses correctly. Young founders have fewer opportunities to learn how to build a gigantic, global enterprise and what to do when a competitor launches an innovation. Of course, skill and ability played a role in Google's success story, but in reality, luck played a bigger part than the description suggests. The greater the share of luck in a story, the less can be learned from it. The powerful WYSIATI rule is to blame. It forces us to deal with the limited information we have as if that is all we can know about the subject. From the sparse information we then construct the best possible story that seems logical to us. Paradoxically, it is easier to construct a coherent story if we know little (see

WYSIATI rule).

The book "The Halo Effect: . . . and the Eight Other Business Delusions That Deceive Managers " by Phil Rosenzweig shows that success and failure of managers and executives is overestimated, and their message is rarely useful. For example, the book's blurb (excerpt) states: "When a company's sales and profits increase, there is a strong temptation to suspect a brilliant strategy, a visionary leader, particularly capable employees or an extraordinary corporate culture behind it. If performance declines, the misguided strategy, the arrogant management style, the uncommitted employees or the uninspired corporate culture are soon pilloried. Hardly anything has changed - except perception".

We gladly believe what the media present to us or what experts and gurus have to say about cryptocurrencies. The "social proof", i.e., the number of likes, followers etc., additionally influences our perception of this person. Later we will still see with the "Illusion of competence" that this is mostly unjustified. Since people are basically lazy and do not check the quality of the information themselves, they are thus strongly influenced by what they say, which in turn negatively influences their investment decisions.

To counteract the halo effect, we can apply the "multiple-eye principle". The multiple-eye principle is a preventive control in which several people assess the decisions or actions of one person. A further measure is an assessment of a person's decisions and actions that is as objective as possible. In addition, we should sensitize our own perception and resort to more self-reflection. We should judge the characteristics of a person individually and not let ourselves be tempted by an "outshined" characteristic to other characteristics or the overall impression. We should also not be blinded by the number of likes or followers.

Illusion of competence: Why experts do not make better predictions

The illusion of skill is the belief that competent people can make better predictions. This is particularly widespread in politics, business and the stock market.

What makes an investor buy shares that another investor sells? What does the buyer think he knows that the seller does not? Most traders know that they have the same information and exchange shares because they have different opinions. Buyers think the stock is undervalued and the price will go up, while sellers think the stock is overvalued and the price should go down. Both believe that the current price is unreasonable. Why do both think they know the price better than the market? The truth is that many investors consistently make losses and are therefore worse than when shares are picked at random. An entire industry seems to be based on an illusion of competence. This is also true for the crypto-market.

In a study by Terry Odean, data from transactions of individual investors over a period of 7 years with over 10,000 accounts and over 163,000 buy and sell transactions were analyzed. The result was that on average, the stocks the traders sold performed significantly better than those they bought. On average, the return was 3.2% per year better, considering transaction costs. So, it would have been better for the majority of investors to do nothing but follow their ideas. In a study by Odean and Brad Barber entitled: "Securities transactions threaten your assets", they showed that the most active traders had the worst results, while the passive ones achieved the highest returns.

Every securities transaction has a business partner, such as professional investors and financial institutions, who are willing to exploit the mistakes of private investors in their actions. Much research has looked closely at the mistakes made by private investors. Private investors tend to sell winning shares, i.e., shares that have risen in price since the purchase. On the other hand, they hold on to their loser shares. Unfortunately for them, however, in the short-term winner shares show a better performance than the loser shares. This means that investors sold the wrong shares and bought the wrong ones. Private investors are also much more susceptible to news. They turn to companies that predictably attract their attention with headlines. Professional investors react much more selectively to news (see also availability errors).

Financial professionals who professionally manage investors' money gave themselves the name "Smart Money". But very few have the knowledge and skills consistently to beat the market year after year. In vain, one looks for lasting success with professional investors and fund managers. The decisive criterion for competence (and therefore success) is consistency. This would mean that the annual ranking of investors and funds should not fluctuate randomly, and that the correlation of rankings should not be zero from year to year. The data situation after 50 years of research is clear: for the vast majority of fund managers, the selection of individual securities resembles a game of dice and, in general, the performance of two out of three investment funds in any given year is worse than that of the overall market. It is also interesting to note that the correlation between consecutive annual investment results is virtually zero. The successful funds in any given year were simply luckier. But the most remarkable thing is that even if the directors or owners of funds are confronted with the reality that their fund managers are just playing a game of chance, they do nothing about it. This statistical information is ignored if it contradicts the impressions from personal experience. Facts that question basic assumptions (e.g., fund managers do not consistently generate better returns than the market) and thus threaten people's livelihood and self-esteem are simply ignored. This also applies to stock pickers. Only a few of them know it, but stock pickers play just as much of a game of chance. Securities traders subjectively have the feeling of making rational, well-founded decisions in a situation of great uncertainty. Unfortunately, in the markets, educated guesses are not more accurate than random guesses. Studies have confirmed that people who earn their living by thoroughly studying a particular subject area make worse predictions than randomly selected options. Interestingly, even in the area where they were most knowledgeable, they were not significantly better than non-experts. Respected experts tend to overestimate themselves more than their colleagues, rarely admit mistakes to themselves, and always have an appropriate excuse.

All too often, we rely on so-called experts for our investment decisions. One reason for this is that we do not want to do the work ourselves to arrive at a good decision and therefore prefer to rely on experts. One problem is that people pay attention to the "social status" of experts. This usually means that the more ratings, likes or followers a person has, the more likely he or she is to be considered an "expert". Unfortunately, ratings, likes or followers are no guarantee for expertise at all. Never trust an expert. They are not aware of their misjudgments. Experts show many of the same distortions that we mere mortals do. Their risk assessments and preferences often differ from those of other people.

Insight illusion: Why you should not read success stories

Insight illusions arise because we tend to reverse causal relationships due to the halo effect. We think that companies fail because the boss is too inflexible. But it is the other way around. The truth is that the boss seems inflexible because the company's business is going badly. Another example of cognitive illusions are books that try to derive concrete courses of action from systematic investigations of successful companies or personalities. The halo effect (see chapter 3) and the outcome bias both explain the extraordinary success of such books. One of the most famous examples is the book "Built to Last: Successful Habits of Visionary Companies" by Jim Collins and Jerry I. Porras. The key message of this and similar books is that good management practices can be identified, and good results can be achieved. Both assertions are exaggerated, because the comparison of companies that have been more or less successful, is for the most part, a comparison of companies that have been more or less lucky. If chance plays along, regular patterns can only be illusions (see clustering illusion).

Unbelievable stories about the rise and fall of companies or personalities are listened to by readers because they offer what people need: A simple message of victory and defeat that identifies clear causes. Unfortunately, ignorance often obscures the power of chance and thus the inevitability of regression (see chapter 6). Therefore, all these stories create an illusion of "understanding" and make the reader believe that he has learned some important lessons. However, this is demonstrably not the case. We would like to hear the success stories of traders or investors who have come to great wealth and want to apply their "recipes for success". Most of the time, however, luck played a much, much greater role than they did and what we want to believe.

Overconfidence-bias: Why CFOs can't predict the price

When I built up my mining company, I had a lot of contact with other mining operators to exchange information about the business and other opportunities in this industry. One of the miners was engaged in speculative mining (mining is the mining of cryptocurrencies). In speculative mining one looks for still unknown cryptocurrencies and is one of the first to mine them. Since one begins early, one can generate a very large number of cryptocurrencies in a short time. One speculates on the fact that the project grows and thus, also the price of the prospected cryptocurrency rises, in order to sell (dump) it then at a good time on the market. He had a good hand for this and always boasted of his perfect analyses and prophecies, which led to the prospecting of this or that cryptocurrency. Later, when he had to take some setbacks, it turned out that much was just luck and he was subject to "overestimation of himself".

The overconfidence-bias (or overconfidence effect) is a form of systematic misjudgment of one's own abilities and knowledge as well as one's own competencies and follows from the WYSIATI rule. Neither the quality nor the quantity of information influences our decisions. The extent of what we believe depends largely on the story we make up from the limited information. We do not consider that we have too little information to form a good judgment. We therefore believe we can do more, know more, hold out longer or have more influence than we actually do. Overestimation of our own abilities is usually contextual. People tend to underestimate their abilities in difficult tasks and overestimate them in simple tasks (such as driving a car). It is also noteworthy that on average women tend to overestimate their abilities less than men.

Optimism is widespread, persistent and costly. In a study, chief financial officers of large corporations were asked to predict the average return of the S&P 500 (Standard & Poor's share index of the 500 largest listed U.S. companies) for the following year. The result of the 11,600 predictions collected was clear. The CFOs had no idea how the index would develop in the short term. The correlation between the actual development and the predictions was just below zero. This means that when the board members predicted falling prices, they tended to rise. The problem with these not surprising results, however, is that the CFOs did not know that their predictions were worthless. In addition to the performance of the S&P 500, respondents had to make two other estimates. One, which they felt was too high with 90 percent certainty and the second, which was too low with 90 percent certainty. This range is referred to in the statistics as the 80 percent confidence interval. Results outside this range are outliers (i.e., 20 percent of results). In such experiments there were far too many outliers. The frequency was 67 percent, which was more than three times as much as expected. This means that CFOs greatly overestimated their ability to predict the market. Overestimation is another proof of the WYSIATI rule. When we need to predict or estimate something, we rely on the information that comes to us spontaneously and use it to construct a coherent story that makes our estimate seem reasonable. It is almost impossible for us to take into account information that we do not know. The authors of the study then calculated the frequencies of outliers back to the required 20 percent. The result was then: The performance of the S&P 500 will be between minus 10 percent and plus 30 percent next year with 80 percent probability. However, a CFO would never say this.

So, in general, we construct a story about a share price performance based on the little information we have available at the moment. We do not consider other possible events and therefore overestimate our ability to predict the price trend.

CHAPTER 4: Why losses are more painful than gains are gratifying

The prospect theory: Decisions under uncertainty

The new prospect theory was presented in 1979 by the two psychologists Daniel Kahneman and Amos Tversky as an alternative to the expectation-utility theory. In utility theory, probabilities and decision weights are identical. A rationally thinking person would therefore always choose the option that produces the best expected value. However, we know from research that this is not the case. The prospect theory establishes the real relationship between probability and decision weight. To understand the prospect theory, take a look at the following examples:

Example 1: What do you choose?
   a)   receive $900 safely or
   b)   a 90 percent chance to win $1000?
Write down your answer!

Example 2: What do you choose?
   a)   A safe loss of $900 or
   b)   a 90 percent probability of losing $1000?
Write down your answer!

The majority of respondents are risk averse in example 1 and therefore choose answer a). The subjective value of a safe $900 is greater than a 90 percent chance of winning $1000. In example 2, most people decide to take the risk and choose answer b). The subjective value of a loss of $900 is much greater than the 90 percent chance of losing $1000. The safe loss creates a strong feeling of risk avoidance and induces people to take the risk.

Example 3: In addition to your current assets, you will receive $1000. Decide on one of the following options:
   a)   A 50 percent chance to win $1000 or
   b) $500 safely received

Write down your answer!

Example 4: In addition to your current assets, you will receive $2000. Decide on one of the following options:
  a) a 50 percent probability to lose $1000 or
  b) $500 to lose safely
Write down your answer!

Examples 3 and 4 are equivalent in terms of the final state of assets. In both cases you have the choice between two equal options. Either one is definitely $1500 richer than before, or one accepts a gamble in which one will be $1000 or $2000 richer than before with a 50% probability. Nevertheless, the answers differ. In example 3 the majority decided for the safe choice b) and in example 4 however, for the lottery a). The comparison of the examples illustrates the decisive role of the reference point from which the evaluation is made. The reference point is the previous state to which the assessment of winnings and losses refers. In example 3 the reference point is $1000, in example 4 it is $2000. If the final asset value is $1500, it corresponds to a profit of $500 in example 3 and a loss of $500 in example 4.

If you are like most people, you have not paid much attention to the gift of $1000 or $2000 before you made your choice. In fact, there is no reason to pay attention to the gift since reference points are generally ignored.

In the prospect theory, there are the following three characteristics that are central to the evaluation of financial results:

First, the assessment is made in relation to a neutral reference point. The reference point is usually the status quo. However, it can also be an outcome that you expect or an outcome that you think you deserve (for example, a salary increase or a bonus that your colleagues receive). Results that are better than the reference point are considered gains. Results that are worse than the reference point are perceived as losses. To internalize the reference point, you can do the following experiment:

Place three bowls on the table. The two outer ones are filled, one with cold water and one with hot water. The middle one is filled with water at room temperature. Hold one hand in the hot water and the other hand in the cold water for about one minute. Then put both hands in the middle bowl, which is at room temperature. You will see that you will feel the same temperature as the cold water in one hand and warm water in the other.

To illustrate the point of reference for investments, put yourself in the following situation: You are in the profit zone with one position, and shortly after that the price drops. Although you would still make a profit, you will feel that the decrease in profit is a loss because your reference point has automatically moved up with the price.

Secondly, we perceive subjective differences in higher asset levels as much smaller than in lower ones. Consider the following example: The subjective difference between 900 and 1000 dollars is much smaller than the difference between 100 and 200 dollars. In other words, there is a principle of decreasing sensitivities when assessing changes in wealth. This means that differences are perceived as smaller for higher asset values: The difference between 900 and 1000 dollars is perceived as less than the difference between 100 and 200 dollars. In the first case the increase would be only about 11%, whereas in the second case the increase would be 100%. However, in both cases we are 100 dollars richer than before.

Thirdly: The loss aversion. When options are compared directly with each other, losses outweigh gains. This is due to the history of evolution because people who act more cautiously have a higher chance of survival. We are more afraid of losses than we are happy about profits. On average, a loss has an emotional impact twice as strong as an equivalent gain. A loss position of $1000 causes much more emotional pain than a profit position of $1000 brings emotional joy (see next chapter).

Loss aversion: Why we deprive ourselves of our profits

Consider the following example:
We flip a coin once. If we toss a number, you lose $100. Heads you win $150. Would you take this gamble? Write down your answer!

The expected benefit of this game of chance is obviously positive because you can win more than you can lose, and yet you will probably refuse this game. Most people reject this gamble because the fear of losing $100 is greater than the hope of winning $150. Kahneman and Tversky concluded from many such observations that people value losses more highly than profits and are therefore afraid of losing. In other words, people are generally angrier about a loss of $100 than they are happy about a gain of $150. In several experiments, the loss aversion rate of people was tested. They were asked at what winning amount they would respond to the winning game. The loss aversion rate averages between 1.5 and 2.5. Some people have a stronger loss aversion than others. To measure the strength of your loss aversion, ask yourself the following question:

What is the lowest profit you need to make up for the 50% probability of losing $100? In other words: How much do you want to win at least to play this game of chance? Write down your answer!

For many people, the answer is about twice the amount of the loss, about $200. From this you can calculate the loss aversion rate. The formula is:

$$\text{Loss aversion rate} = \frac{\text{amount of profit}}{\text{amount of loss}}$$

Professional investors in the financial markets are more tolerant of losses, and therefore have a lower loss aversion rate. Assumptions suggest that they do not react emotionally to every small fluctuation. In a test with test persons who were told to think like a securities trader, the loss aversion decreased. The test subjects' physical reactions to emotional excitement were measured and it was seen that their emotional response to losses decreased significantly.

To test their loss aversion rate, consider the following questions. Try to ignore all social considerations and try not to be bold or cautious. Focus solely on your subjective perception of the potential loss and compensatory gain.

We consider a game of chance with a 50% probability of winning (as in the previous coin flip example) where you can lose $10. It is only thrown once. What is the smallest win that makes this bet attractive for you? Write down the number!

If your answer is $10, you are indifferent to the risk. Your loss aversion rate is exactly 1. If your answer is less than $10, you are prepared to take risks. Your loss aversion rate is less than 1. If your answer is greater than $10, you are risk averse. Your loss aversion rate is greater than 1. Now consider the following examples:

Again, it is about a single coin toss. This time the possible loss is $500. What potential win do you want to have to play this game? Write down your answer!

What about a possible loss of $2000? What potential win do you want to have? Write down your answer!

Now, if you look at the answers and calculate the loss aversion rate, you will probably find that your loss aversion rate tends to increase as the stakes increase. Of course, with potential ruinous losses, the loss aversion rate is very high. There are some risks that people simply won't take, no matter how big the profit is. This is especially true when existence or lifestyle is threatened.

The following two principles can be derived from experiments on loss aversion: First, in a game of chance where both a win and a loss are possible (this is also called a "mixed lottery"), loss aversion leads to risk-averse behavior. Since losses are experienced much more intensively than winnings of the same amount, people always try to avoid losses. This leads to the fact that we are tempted to invest in "safe" investments and thus miss out on long-term profits, or that, for example, if prices fall for a short time, we exit the position too early for fear of making losses. Secondly, with the two choices A: more probable, higher loss and B: safer, lower loss, people generally behave in a risk-averse manner and choose option A. In this case, the loss is valued about twice as high as the potential gain. A loss of $900 hedged weights more heavily than 90 percent of a loss of $1000. These two findings are the quintessence of the prospect theory developed by Daniel Kahneman and Amos Tversky.

If you invest in Bitcoin or other cryptocurrencies, you should do so based on a long-term strategy and not pay attention to daily fluctuations. Ideally, you should not look at the price on a daily basis. If you observe the price less frequently, you will perceive fewer losses (as long as the basic trend is positive). Evaluations of investors have shown that long-term investors achieve higher returns because they are not frightened by unrealized losses.

The disposition effect: Why we lose returns when we sell winners

Consider the following example:

Imagine you are a securities trader and have a stock portfolio. You need money and therefore have to sell shares. You remember the price at which you bought the shares and can sell shares at either a profit or a loss. Stock G is a winner with a $5000 profit. Share V is a loser. The price of both shares has remained stable in the last weeks. Which share are you more likely to sell?
Write down your answer!

A legitimate formulation for this decision problem could be: "I could sell G-share and have a $5000 profit on my investment balance sheet. I could also sell stock V and have to record a loss, i.e., a failure. What should I do?" The way the problem is formulated, it is a choice between joy (make a profit) and anger (make a loss) and you are more likely to sell the winning G-share and be happy about your excellent investment decisions. This distortion is called the disposition effect. The disposition effect is the tendency of investors to sell positions that have increased in value and to hold positions that have decreased in value. It is also interesting that the disposition effect was not only found among private investors and day traders, but also among professional and institutional investors and investment funds. The effect is a case of "tight framing", which means that the investor has set up a separate (mental) account for each share he has bought, and he wants to close each one with a profit. This creates a good feeling, but you pay for it. A rational investor would have a comprehensive overview of the entire portfolio and would sell the stock that is least likely to perform well in the future, without considering whether it is a winner or a loser. If you care more about your assets than your emotions, you should act just like a rational investor and sell the loser V and keep the winner G. Realizing losses will also reduce your tax burden, while selling winners will give you additional taxes.

This is known to all investors when they think about their tax return in December, and then they are more likely to shed losers. This "tax advantage" is available all year round, but for the remaining 11 months mental accounting unfortunately, prevails over common financial sense. At least with shares there is another reason against selling winners. This is the well-documented market anomaly in which shares that have risen recently are likely to continue to rise at least for a short time. Whether there is such a market anomaly with cryptocurrencies has not yet been investigated.

Certainty effect and possibility effect: How lotteries and insurance companies rip us off

Consider the following example: *The chance of receiving one million USD increases by five percent each time.*

 a) *The probability increases from 0 to 5 percent.*
 b) *The probability increases from 5 to 10 percent.*
 c) *The probability increases from 60 to 65 percent.*
 d) *The probability increases from 95 to 100 percent.*

What do you think about these probabilities? Which change impresses you? Which one does not? Write down your answers!

Bernoulli's expectation principle says that our benefit increases by exactly 5 percent. However, this is not the case in reality, as you have probably discovered yourself. An increase from 0 percent to 5 percent is more impressive than from 5 percent to 10 percent or from 60 percent to 65 percent. A change from 0 percent to 5 percent is a fundamental change. There is now a possibility to win something that did not exist before. This is a qualitative change, while the change from 5 percent to 10 percent is only a quantitative change. Although the change from 5 percent to 10 percent doubles the probability of winning, we feel that the psychological value of the expectation of winning does not double. The possibility effect is illustrated by the strong effect from 0 percent to 5 percent. It ensures that highly unlikely outcomes are disproportionately overweighted. An example of this is people who are prepared to pay a large price for very small chances, as is the case with lottery tickets, for example. The certainty effect, on the other hand, comes into play when there is an improvement from 95 percent to 100 percent. Results that are almost certain are weighted less than their probability justifies. Consider the following example to illustrate the certainty effect:

Imagine that you have inherited one million USD. Someone in the family disputes the will in court. Your lawyer assures you that the law is on your side and that the probability of winning is 95 percent. But he also says that court decisions are never 100 percent predictable. The case will be heard in court tomorrow. Today, however, an underwriting firm approaches you and would immediately buy the case for $910,000. Which one do you choose? Do you accept the underwriting company's offer, or do you prefer to go to court? Write down your answer!

The offer of the risk company is $40,000 lower than the expected value of the judgement (see also chapter 7: Calculate expected values), which is $950,000 (1,000,000 * 0.95 = 950,000). If you should ever get into such a situation, keep in mind that there is a whole industry for structured settlements that offer "security" at a high price and take advantage of the security effect.

The Allais paradox

The Allais paradox was named after Maurice Allais, a French engineer and scientist who was awarded the Nobel Prize for Economics for his groundbreaking contributions to the theory of markets and the efficient use of resources. In an experiment during a lecture, he asked his audience a series of questions about decision making. Allais wanted to show his guests that they were vulnerable to the security effect, that they were not making rational decisions and that this violated the theory of expected utility. Example of a simplified version of the Allais problem:

Problem A: Choose between
  1. *a 61 percent chance of winning $520,000 or*
  2. *a 63 percent chance to win $500,000*
Which of the two options do you choose? Write down your answer!

Problem B: Choose between
  1. *a 98 percent chance of winning $520,000 or*
  2. *a 100 percent chance to win $500,000*
Which of the two options do you choose? Write down your answer!

If you are like most people, then you chose answer 1 for problem A and answer 2 for problem B. If these were your answers, then you have violated the rules of rational decision making and committed a logical sin. To illustrate the problem, consider the following: Imagine the result is determined by blindly drawing from an urn with 100 balls. If you draw a red ball, you win; if you draw a white one, you lose. For problem A, almost all respondents preferred urn 1, although it contains fewer winning red balls (only 61 balls instead of 63 in urn 2), because the difference in winning ($20,000 more profit) is more tempting than the difference in probability. For problem B, the vast majority of respondents chose urn 2, which guarantees a $500,000 profit. But this is a logical mistake. If you take a closer look at the two urns of problem B, you will see that the urns are better versions of the two urns of problem A. In version B, 37 white balls per urn were simply exchanged for winning red balls (61+37=98 in urn 1 and 63+37=100 in urn 2). The improvement in the first urn is clearly greater than the improvement in the second, because each red ball gives you another chance to win the $520,000 in urn 1, while you can only win $500,000 in urn 2. In problem

A you chose urn 1, which was then improved more than urn 2, and yet you chose the worse, urn 2. This logically unwise decision can be explained psychologically by the safety effect. The two percent difference between a 100 percent and a 98 percent chance of winning in problem B is much more impressive than the two percent difference from 61 percent to 63 percent in problem A. The respondents thus violate the utility theory. People are not rational decision-makers, we do not decide according to the benefit theory.

The possibility effect and certainty effect have a similarly strong impact not only on profits, but also on losses. The possibility effect makes us overrate small risks and we are willing to pay a lot of money (much more than the expected value) to eliminate this small risk. Consider the following situation: If a family member is operated on, a five percent risk of amputation is bad. Compared to a 10% risk, it is much more than half as bad. The safety effect, on the other hand, means that large risks are underestimated. Consider the following situation: The hope that a 95 percent catastrophe will not occur and the certainty that a catastrophe will occur is disproportionately high. The overweighting of very high probabilities increases the attractiveness of gambling and insurance.

Result: The weight of a decision that people attribute to high and low probability outcomes contradicts the expectation principle. The decision weights are not identical with the probabilities of these results. With the possibility effect unlikely results are overweighted. With the safety effect very probable results are underweighted in relation to their actual occurrence security.

The problem here is however, that a decision maker who wants to be rational, must submit to the expectation principle. This means that we must weight the utility values according to their probability. In other words: We must eliminate the security and possibility effect. In the table below you will find a summary of the certainty effect and the possibility effect.

	Profit	Loss
High probability **Certainty effect** Results that are almost certain are underweighted in relation to their probability	95% chance to win $100,000 Risk-averse behavior People don't want to take risks; they prefer to accept a safer but lower offer. Fear of disappointment nothing to gain	95% chance to lose $100,000 Risk taking behavior hope to avoid a high loss.
Low probability **Possibility effect** Unlikely results are disproportionately overweighted	5% chance to win $100.000 Risk taking behavior People are willing to pay a high price for small opportunities. Hope for profit	5% chance to lose $100,000 Risk-averse behavior Fear of great loss. Small risks are overrated. People pay a high price to eliminate risk.

CHAPTER 5: Emotions and feelings. Influence on our investment decisions

Affect heuristic: Our feelings and emotions decide

I remember the following drastic day trading situation. I had made some good trades and was in a good mood. I opened another position and then had to take my car to the garage for an annual check. When I took a quick look at my cell phone in the workshop to pass the time, I saw that my position was massively negative. Suddenly, my pulse jumped up and I started to sweat. I was in the workshop and could not go home to my computer to close the position manually. I noticed how I was getting more and more nervous the further the price fell. A feeling of powerlessness was added as I had to wait until the car's inspection was being finished. My mood took a turn for the worse, which also caught the attention of the people in the workshop. I could no longer take my eyes off my smartphone and stared at the price falling further and further. I drove home as fast as possible and closed the position. Just as I was trying to process the loss (at that time the easiest thing to do was to "push it away"), the price reversed and climbed back up again. I asked myself: "What an idiot, why did I close the position? If I had waited, I would have made fewer losses." Now my negative mood was compounded by anger and regret. In the end the position was far in my original direction. If I had done nothing and just waited, I could have closed the position with a profit. A quick look at my smartphone changed everything. My feelings and emotions took over my thinking. I fell into a kind of panic and all actions were driven by these feelings and emotions. I was not in control of the situation. This is the extreme form of affect heuristics.

Affect heuristic means that we consult our mood, feelings and emotions when making judgments and decisions. We ask ourselves: Do I like it? Do I not like it? How strongly do I react emotionally? What mood am I in right now? In many areas of life, people form opinions and make decisions related to their feelings without knowing that they are doing so. Affect heuristics is a case of substitution where our brain replaces a difficult question such as "What do I think about it" with the easier question "What feelings does it arouse in me". The problem, however, is that we do not consciously notice this substitution itself. In terms of cryptocurrencies this could look like this: We answer the difficult question "Should I invest in Bitcoin" instead with the easier question "Do I like Bitcoin?" without noticing this replacement. Results from studies have shown that test persons ascribe a greater benefit and a lower risk to a technology if they had a positive attitude towards the technology. If they did not like the technology, the disadvantages far outweighed the benefits. In terms of cryptocurrencies, this means that investors are more likely to invest in a cryptocurrency if they have an affinity with the technology. In addition, it plays a role, as to how an investor stands emotionally in relation to a project and its use case. Depending on emotions, feelings and mood, buying and selling is influenced more or less strongly. Emotions and feelings when trading and investing can very quickly lead to irrational decisions. Therefore, we have to become aware of our emotions and feelings and eliminate them to a large extent. In principle, a longer investment horizon and less frequent observation of the market are highly effective against too strong emotions and feelings.

Typical emotions we encounter when trading and investing:
- Fear of losing money if the trade/investment goes bad
- Increased fear of losing money in the investment when it is needed elsewhere (e.g., to pay back debts, cover living expenses, repair the car, etc.)
- Greed, for example, to not get out of a position because you think you will make even more profit
- Disappointment of having made an investment that you were sure would be a winner

- Remorse for having made a decision that turned out to be bad
- Euphoria or strong optimism when a few trades or investments are going well

Regret: Why we regret some investments, but do not have to do so

We are afraid of making an investment decision that we will regret later. We often hear about in our environment: "Don't do this, you'll regret it!" Regret is an emotion and also a form of punishment that we inflict on ourselves. It goes along with this feeling that one should have known better. We struggle with thoughts about the mistakes we made by making the wrong decision and the opportunities that were missed. We have a deep desire to undo this mistake and try to correct the mistake and get a second chance. If we can imagine that someone could have acted differently, we usually experience intense regret. Regret is an emotion that does not correspond to reality and is only triggered by the availability of alternatives. If there was only one way we could behave, we would not feel remorse. Put yourself in the following position:

Paul is an equity investor. He invests in cryptocurrencies for the first time and loses part of his assets. George often invests in cryptocurrencies and loses part of his fortune. Who will regret the situation more? Write down your answer!

Which of them will be criticized more by third parties? Write down your answer!

In a similar experiment, the majority of the respondents said that Paul will regret it more. In contrast, the majority of the respondents criticized George more than Paul. Regret and criticism are different. The emotions of Paul and George differ and are determined by how they usually invest. For Paul it is a rare (or unusual) event, so people expect him to feel a stronger sense of remorse. An observer is more likely to criticize George for taking disproportionate risks, whereas Paul was simply unlucky. However, Paul is the person who will be more annoyed because he behaved atypically in this one situation. This example illustrates the general pattern that people show stronger emotional reactions (including remorse) to an outcome that comes about through "doing". Conversely, we have weaker emotional responses to the same outcome when it comes from "not doing" (inaction). This has also been confirmed with gambling. People are more satisfied when they play risky games and win than when they did not play a game of chance and simply received the same amount of money. The decisive factor here is not the difference between "doing" and "not doing" but the difference between standard options and actions that deviate from the standard. The default option for Paul is not to invest in cryptocurrencies. Investing in cryptocurrencies is a deviation from the standard option and is associated with regret. The effect of deviating from the default option illustrates the following situation: The default option is to greet your family when they come to visit at the weekend. Deviating from the default option means not welcoming the family and this is likely to lead to remorse and criticism.

Another example of remorse:

Peter possesses cryptocurrency A. In the last year he considered whether he should change to cryptocurrency B. But he decided against it. Now he learns that he would be $1200 richer if he had switched to B.

Ben was in possession of cryptocurrency B. Last year he exchanged it for cryptocurrency A. He now learns that he would have been $1200 richer if he had kept cryptocurrency B.

Who regrets his behavior more? Write down your answer!

In a similar experiment, only 8 percent of the respondents said that Peter would regret his behavior. 92 percent of the respondents said that Ben would regret it more. This is strange because objectively speaking, the situations of the two are the same. Both own cryptocurrency A and both would be $1200 richer if they owned cryptocurrency B. The difference is that Ben got into this situation by acting, while Peter got into the same situation by not acting. The default option for the cryptocurrency owner is to keep the cryptocurrency and not to sell it. Selling the cryptocurrency is a deviation from the standard option and therefore a candidate for remorse.

Another example: Sometimes we make an investment decision with which we do not feel one hundred percent comfortable. Some inner voice tells us that we should not do it. If the investment then turns out positive, we are glad we made that decision. If, on the other hand, the investment turns out negative, we will feel great remorse. We have the option of either not making an investment that we do not feel comfortable with, or we have to be aware that we may regret this decision before making the investment. The most useful thing to do before making a decision is to go into detail about the expectation of regret. If something goes wrong and you can remember that you carefully considered the possibility of repentance before making the decision, you will probably experience less repentance. Remorse occurs together with the regression error. The error of repentance can therefore additionally strengthen the feeling of remorse. Therefore, use a journal for every investment decision and enter all factors, thoughts, feelings and emotions regarding the investment in it.

Put yourself in the following situations before investing:
   a)   You spend a lot of time and are thorough in your decision making
   b)   You are completely unconcerned and decidedly simply

spontaneous

c)   You spend some time and think a little about the decision
Which of the situations will you regret more? Which of them will you
regret less? Write down your answer!

You should regret situations a) and b) only slightly or not at all. In a) you have done everything in your power to come to a good decision. In b) you deliberately did not make any effort to make a decision. You knew that you were going to gamble. With c), however, you will feel remorse because you made small efforts and think that you might have made a better decision if you had spent more time and energy on it. Conclusion: When deciding with long-term consequences, you should either be very thorough or completely unconcerned. Looking back is worse when you are just thinking a little. Just enough that you have to tell yourself later: I almost made a better decision.

Disappointment: Why we do not have to be disappointed by some investments

Example: Consider the following profit expectations:
   a)   A one-in-a-million chance to win one million USD.
   b)   A 90 percent chance of winning $17 and a 10 percent chance
       of winning nothing.
   c)   A 90 percent chance of winning one million USD and a 10
       percent chance of winning nothing.

Which option would you be most disappointed in? Write down your answer!

For all three options, "win nothing" is a possible event and equally likely (10% probability). So, the starting point (reference point) is "win nothing" and its value is zero. However, this does not correspond to our experience. In cases

a) and b), "win nothing" is a non-event and it makes sense to assign it a value of zero. In option c), however, it is very disappointing not to win anything because the high probability sets a new reference point, and we experience it as a loss to win nothing. This is a problem for the prospect theory because it does not allow the value of a result, in this case "gain nothing", to change. In other words, the prospect theory cannot represent disappointments although they exist in reality. Repentance is also not considered by the theory.

Put yourself in the following situation: You have the following choices:

a) Choose between a 90 percent chance of winning 1 million USD and a 100 percent chance of winning $50.
b) Choose between a 90 percent chance of winning 1 million USD and a 100 percent chance of winning $150,000.

Now compare the mental pain you would feel if you chose to win in both cases but did not win. In the first case it is also disappointing not to win anything, but the potential pain in b) is made worse by knowing that you have acted greedily. Not having chosen the safe $150,000, one deeply regrets this. Various psychologists and economists have proposed models for decision making that reflect emotions such as remorse or disappointment. The problem is that these theories make only a few accurate predictions and therefore could not prevail over the prospect theory.

Why should we not be disappointed? When we invest, we will not even come close to a 100% hit rate. Losses are part of investing. Think like a professional securities trader and internalize the following mantra: "Sometimes you lose, sometimes you win".

Fear and greed: Impact on our investment decisions

Some of my worst Bitcoin investments have to do with fear and greed. One was in January 2017 when the Bitcoin price collapsed from just under $1200, I sold all my Bitcoin positions at $800 out of fear and panic. The price dropped to about $750 and then rose to almost $1400. Another one was when the Bitcoin price reached its all-time high of almost $20,000 at the end of 2017 and I did not sell because I was obsessed by greed and hoped for further price increases.

Emotions influence our trading and investment decisions. Especially fear and greed are two strong emotions that guide our decisions. We feel fear when we are threatened. For example, when we are wandering in the Savannah hunting for food and suddenly a big cat crosses our paths. In such a situation we should have evolutionary anxiety. It is a natural instinct to ensure our survival. Greed could be our death sentence, if we simply continue to hunt carelessly, we will probably be eaten by the big cat. Loss trades are threats that cause fear because we lose money. We do not like to lose. Greed is also firmly anchored in us. The best chances of survival were for those who had the most resources, such as food, clothing and tools. Fear and greed are therefore always present in us due to evolution. Greed works against fear. If we are too afraid, then we would probably not go hunting at all and would starve. So, greed and fear are important for our survival. In principle, these are the following four ways in which fear and greed affect an open position:

	Fear	Greed
Profit position	Fear that profits will decrease	Hope for even greater profits
Loss position	Fear of even greater losses	Hope for price reversal and profits

Imagine you had a position open overnight, and in the morning you see that the position is in loss. Depending on the level of your fear and greed, your loss aversion rate and the size of the position that is in loss, you will feel more or less discomfort. In this situation, we are afraid of even greater losses on the one hand, and hope that the price will turn around and we will make profits on the other. Now imagine that you opened a position overnight, and in the morning you see that the position is in profit. Depending on your level of fear and greed, your loss aversion rate and the size of the position that is in profit, you will feel more or less joy. In this situation, however, the fear that the profit could be reduced often reappears and on the other hand, our greed drives us to leave the position open further in order to make even bigger profits. It is extremely unpleasant when we are in a loss position. But it is also unpleasant when our own greed causes us to close an original winning position at a loss.

In such situations it is valuable to "feel" how our emotions influence our decisions. For every investor or trader, there comes a point in his or her career when panic reactions occur, leading to bad decisions. In these situations, our emotions take over our thinking and we often behave irrationally. It is important that we learn from this. The first step to get a grip on these reactions is to have actually experienced the emotions. Only those who know how it feels and how uncontrolled we act through it can react correctly and act better the next time. The most important thing is that we are aware when we become emotional and fear or greed takes over our thinking. In such a situation, it is good to look within oneself and make sure not to make hasty decisions driven by emotions. We must now focus on the facts and evaluate the situation rationally. We should briefly distance ourselves from what is happening. It is especially important to remain calm and patient, because under haste one usually makes bad decisions. Haste leads us to let fear and greed take control. In such a situation, take your journal and write down what you feel, what decision you are going to make and what the reasons for that decision are. You will find that the process of writing it down already helps you make better decisions.

The availability cascade: How hype and crashes are triggered

The availability cascade is a self-sustaining chain of events. It usually starts with media reports about a relatively insignificant event, leads to public attention and finally to massive media coverage. The sequence is usually as follows: A media report attracts the attention of a part of the public, which is thereby shaken up (in case of positive events) or disturbed (in case of negative events). These emotions then become a story in themselves, which triggers further media coverage, causing even greater optimism (for positive events) or concern (for negative events). This cycle is then gladly accelerated by "availability companies" (which can be individuals or organizations). They work to spread and maintain a steady flow of positive or negative news. The more lurid the headlines, the more the opportunity or risk is overstated. In addition, people have a tendency to neglect probabilities and this leads to exaggerated reactions because the facts of the situation can usually not be assessed correctly.

People buy utopian prices because they are "afraid" to miss something. "Fear of missing out" (FOMO) is the term for this. In addition, it can happen that other investors do not sell out of greed, because the already high profit is still too little for them. This results in a further rise in the share price. Then the hype comes to an end. The first ones take their profits, which slows down the upward trend. Other investors see this, and they may be afraid that their profits will decrease again and therefore sell. This leads to a cascade effect and the price collapses. The previously made profits become smaller and smaller. Now hope comes into play. Some investors think that the share price will only collapse for a short time and then continue to rise. Then it happens that all profits are lost again and possibly even a loss must be recorded.

In addition, FUD can occur at the top of a hype or also in "normal" market events. FUD stands for "Fear, Uncertainty and Doubt". Usually, fear is spread on social media or other channels when prices are falling, which leads to uncertainty and doubts among investors, who then close positions or do not invest, which can lead to a further price slump. The greater the emotions and the more negative the media reports, the more likely it is that falling prices will increase.

How do you recognize hype? To recognize a Hype is not completely simple since our own greed makes us "blind" to it. Some signs that we are in a Hype can be:

- Many media and newspapers write about it and thereby drive the Hype still additionally.
- New price highlights and profits are reached daily.
- Non-linear price increase in the price chart.
- Rising trading volume with rising price and maximum volume at the price peak.
- People who have nothing to do with the respective asset class and are not familiar with it also buy.
- Decoupling of real economy and price.
- Overvalued companies that make neither turnover nor profit.
- Google search queries for the respective cryptocurrency are at a maximum.
- Investors are "afraid" to miss something (Fear of missing out).
- Uncertainty and FUD grows, the higher the price rises.

Ego-Depletion: Why you should not make investment decisions in the evening

After countless bad trades and investment decisions, I began to carefully write down every trade and investment I made in a journal. I wrote down all of the information that led to my investment decision. I documented how I felt before opening, during and after closing positions, and what emotions I felt. After some time, I evaluated all the collected data and saw that the performance of the investments I made in the evening was on average worse than the positions I took in the morning. What was the reason for this? The explanation lies in the so-called "ego-depletion".

Ego-depletion (from Latin ego 'I' and neo-Latin *depletio* 'bloodletting', to deplore 'emptying'; here in the sense of "self-exhaustion") is self-exhaustion through physical, cognitive or emotional effort. All these activities draw energy from a pool. The result is, that logical decision making is worse after an effort. When you are exhausted and hungry, you are looking for the easier solution to a problem and you are not trying hard enough. Also, our ability of self-control depends on our willpower. Willpower is also reduced or even consumed by physical, cognitive or emotional effort, which itself requires willpower. As a result, we have full energy available in the morning and self-exhaustion is at a minimum. During the course of the day, we have to deal with physical, cognitive and emotional exertion, which gradually depletes our pool of energy. In the evening, this energy is as good as used up and we can no longer make good decisions. This energy that is used up can be associated with the consumption of glucose in the brain. Tests have shown that in people who perform self-control tasks, the glucose level in the blood and thus in the brain decreases. Nature follows the law of least effort. This also applies to physical, cognitive or emotional effort. The law says the following: If there are several ways to reach a goal, it will choose the way that involves the least amount of work.

Effort is a cost factor in economics and behind everything there is a balanced cost/benefit ratio. Laziness is therefore deeply rooted in our nature. In English we say "To pay attention" when we focus our attention on something. "To pay" means "to pay something" and this is appropriate because you have a limited attention budget that you can allocate to your activities. If the budget is exceeded, bad decisions are made. The more we try, the less energy is left for good decisions. Also stress, often occurs more with day traders, because they sit for hours in front of the charts, sometimes getting up in the night to trade and end up having bad or short sleep, which consumes their energy and therefore leads to bad decisions.

CHAPTER 6: Statistics and probability

Base rate fallacy: Why neglecting probabilities costs us money

People are not good intuitive statisticians, even statisticians are not good intuitive statisticians. We find it very difficult to estimate statistical values, because our System I is not designed for that. The vast majority does not deal with statistics and probabilities. However, for rational decisions and thus better investment decisions we should at least acquire a minimum of statistics. This includes not neglecting probabilities. Understanding basic principles of statistics and probabilities is important for

- Estimation of the probability of occurrence of events
- Predictions about future events
- Assessment of hypotheses and estimation of frequencies

The base rate fallacy is the neglect of statistical facts. A base rate is the frequency of occurrence of a feature in the population. Examples are the average number of rainy days in a month or the hit rate of a trading system. The following example illustrates this:

What do you think? What is the probability of rain in November? Write down your answer!

You can estimate, but your estimation reliability will be much better if you look at statistical data of rainy days in November. In Vienna there are on average 18 rainy days in November. November has 30 days. To calculate the probability in percent, use the following formula:

$$Probability\ of\ Rain\ [\%] = \frac{18}{\frac{30}{100}} = 60\%$$

You can explain the formula as follows: If it rains 100 percent, then it would have to rain continuously for 30 days. If it rains one percent, simply divide 30 days by 100, so one percent is 0.3 days. If you now divide the 18 rainy days by 0.3, you get 60 percent as a result. So, the probability of rain in November is 60 percent. We should also always look at the opposite probability. With a 60 percent probability of rain, we should also be aware that with a probability of 40 percent (corresponding to 12 days) it will not rain! It is not possible that it will not rain with a probability of 50 percent or 70 percent because the two probabilities of event and non-event together must always add up to 100 percent.

If we neglect simple statistical facts, we have to rely on our estimates. However, as you have already seen in the course of the book, this often causes misjudgments and distortions that have a negative impact on our trading or investment decisions. Therefore, although it may be difficult at first, you should always include statistical facts in your investment and trading decisions.

Many people believe that Bitcoin will quickly reach the $20,000 mark again. The statistical facts are currently as follows: In the entire (over 10 years) life of Bitcoin, it only reached the value of just under $20,000 once. Statistically speaking, this is an outlier.
Some examples of base rates for Bitcoin could be

- What is the probability that Bitcoin will reach $5,000, $10,000, $15,000, $20,000 within one year?
- What is the probability that the Bitcoin price will rise or fall by 5 percent, 10 percent, 15 percent, 20 percent within one day?
- What is the probability that the Bitcoin price will rise or fall by $500, $1000, $2000 within one day?
- What is the probability of a sudden, unexpected event (a so-called Black Swan) that leads to a massive

market collapse (such as the price collapse due to the Corona crisis)?

Take your time and first estimate the probabilities from the above list. Then get the statistical data from the Internet and calculate the probabilities. Compare your estimates with the statistical facts. Use the calculated probabilities as a basis for your next investment decisions.

Availability error: We overestimate what comes to our mind quickly

The availability error, also known as availability heuristic, is the tendency to overestimate the probability of events with higher "availability" in memory. So, we search our memory for information and the more (or the easier) we think of something, the more we estimate it. The influencing factors are: Timeliness of memory, unusualness of the event and the emotional attachment to the event. The more current, unusual and emotional the information is, the easier it is to retrieve. Two reasons why information is easily available are on the one hand, one's own experiences and on the other hand frequent reports in the media. In both cases, one's own emotions also play a role. Through our emotions, which we feel for something, information can be "stored" more easily in the brain. The choice of topics by journalists and our own availability heuristics distort our estimates. The importance of something is judged by how easily (or quickly) something can be retrieved from memory and this is easily determined by the amount of reporting in the media. Frequently occurring topics, attract attention, while other important topics disappear from consciousness because they are not written about. The media and journalists report on what they believe is currently moving the public. Public interest is most easily aroused by dramatic and negative events or stars and starlets. Media exaggerations are widespread, whereas little is written about boring but important topics. Media needs readers to justify themselves to advertisers. The more readers a medium has, the more income can be generated. Therefore, the media must write about what attracts most people and these are usually not the important topics.

We often use availability heuristics unconsciously when the importance or probability of an event needs to be estimated, but we don't take the time or we simply lack the motivation, the will or the possibilities to access precise (e.g., statistical) data. In such cases, our judgment is influenced by how quickly or easily we remember events. The easier or faster we remember something, the more likely we are to judge it. In contrast, we judge events that we remember with difficulty to be less likely. Examples of availability errors are:

- People are taking the train because a plane crashed last month. This is an availability error because the risk of flying has not changed.
- The media hardly ever report on pollutants in the air, so we underestimate their risks.
- We overestimate the risks of a virus because the media constantly report on it.
- Conflicts can arise in projects if someone's contribution to the project is not sufficiently appreciated. The availability error leads to an overestimation of one's own contribution because it is the easiest thing to remember. On the other hand, it is not so easy to remember the cooperation of colleagues and we underestimate their contribution to the project.

We remember the Bitcoin hype in December 2017, when Bitcoin had almost reached the $20,000 mark. This event is easily recalled in our minds, which means that we tend to overestimate the probability of the share price reaching

$20,000 again. In contrast, hardly anyone remembers the Bitcoin hype at the end of November 2013, when Bitcoin had exceeded the $1,000 mark for the first time. Depending on whether some people were invested at the time and made profits or losses, they will remember it better or worse depending on the emotional intensity they experienced (frustration, anger, remorse in the case of losses or joy in the case of profits).

The availability error thus distorts our rational view of good and bad investments. For example, people who have made a bad investment and lost money are more likely to remember it because the loss with the negative emotions sticks "better" in our brain than the positive emotions with profits. The availability error therefore ensures that we are more likely to remember the loss investments than the profitable ones. In addition, with the fear of loss this can even lead to the point that people, for fear of making losses again, no longer invest at all. Caution is also advisable with several successful investments or trades in a row. The availability error ensures that you do not easily remember your failures and makes you overly optimistic, which can lead to misjudgments of your own abilities.

Representativeness heuristics: Do not rely on the obvious

Representativeness heuristic is used to assess the probability of an event occurring under uncertainty. It is a heuristic in which decision makers estimate the probability of events occurring to be higher if they better represent the underlying population. When people rely on representativeness to make judgments, they are likely to judge incorrectly because the fact that something is more representative does not make it more likely. For example, in a coin toss, the sequence head-number-head-number is considered more likely than the sequence to-number-number-number.

Representativeness heuristics can lead to overestimated probability judgments if persons are more strongly influenced in their judgements by concrete (representative) individual information than by base rates or base probabilities.

The heuristic was first described by Kahneman and Tversky. In the so-called "Linda problem", they presented test persons with a description of a woman named Linda. The description contained much about emancipation and Linda's work as a women's rights activist. The test persons were asked whether Linda was a "bank employee" or a "bank employee and feminist". The majority of the test persons estimated the probability that Linda was a "bank employee and feminist" to be higher. However, this is incorrect, because the probability of two events (Linda is a bank employee and Linda is a feminist) cannot be greater than the probability that one of the two events (Linda is a bank employee) will occur alone. Even if all bank employees are feminists, the two probabilities would be equal.

Example of estimates of male body sizes:

There are two samples. One with ten and the second with 1000 measurements. You know that the men measured from the sample are on average 1.70 meters tall.

How likely is it that the respective average of the two samples is exactly 1.70 meters? Write down your answer!

One implication of representativeness heuristics is that people neglect the sample size. Most people give the same probability for both samples in the example above. However, this is an error, since the probability that the sample with the higher number of measurements is exactly 1.70 meters is higher. The mean value of a sample approaches the expected value (1.70

meters) with increasing measurements. Compare this with the coin toss experiment. If you toss a coin only a few times, it may be that it tosses heads or tails all the way through, although the probability of this would have to be 50 percent. Only if you toss the coin very often will the number of heads and tails approximately equalize and in the end the probability will be close to 50%.

Denominator effect: Why we weight probabilities wrongly

Denominator effect means that events with a low probability are weighted much more heavily when they are described in categories of relative frequencies ("how many", e.g., 1 in 100,000 children) than when they are expressed in abstract terms such as opportunities, risks or probabilities ("how probable", e.g., 0.001%).

Example: Two urns
Two urns are filled with red and white balls. If you draw a red ball, you win a prize. Urn A contains 10 balls, one of which is red. Urn B contains 100 balls, 8 of which are red.

Which urn do you take? Write down your answer!

What is interesting about this experiment is that about 35 percent of the respondents take the urn with the larger number instead of the one with the greater chance of winning. The chances of winning are 10 percent (=1/10) in urn A and 8 percent (=8/100) in urn B. This is because attention is paid to the red balls that are likely to win and the number of white balls is not considered carefully enough. These illustrative examples contribute to neglecting the denominator (i.e., not taking the white balls into account).

Example for the illustration of risks:
Illustration 1: The risk of permanent disability when vaccinating children is 0.001 percent.
Illustration 2: One in 100,000 children will be disabled by the vaccination.

Which illustration evokes stronger emotions in you? Write down your answer!

The risk in illustration 1 seems small, whereas in the more vivid illustration 2 an image is evoked in the mind. However, this does not happen in the first statement. The 99,999 children are faded out because we are subject to the denominator effect.

Another example: Consider the following four formulations:

a) In the USA, about 1000 murders are committed annually by people with severe mental illness who do not take their medication.

b) Out of 273 million Americans, 1000 will die this way this year.

c) The probability to be killed by such a person is about 0.00036% per year.

d) Every year 1000 Americans will die this way, less than one-thirtieth of the number of people who die from suicide and one-fourth of the number who die from throat cancer.

Although the information is the same in all 4 representations, we react emotionally differently. This means that we are subject to the framing mentioned earlier. Depending on how the numbers are represented, we react emotionally differently to them. This is not rational behavior and probably leads to wrong decisions.

The correlation-causality error: Everyone who drinks water dies

All people who drink water die. The correlation is given, since all people drink water and also all die at some point. The causality that people die from drinking water is clearly not given. This is the correlation-causality error.

The correlation-causality error (also fallacy of correlation on causality, Latin *Cum hoc ergo propter hoc*) happens, if one confuses pure correlation with causality. Correlation describes a relationship between two or more values. In mathematics, it is designated with "r". The correlation is always a value between -1 and 1, where $r=-1$ means that the two values behave in opposite directions. E.g., Bitcoin increases and Ethereum decreases in the same measure then this would be a correlation of $r=-1$. A correlation of $r=1$ means that the two values behave the same. E.g., Bitcoin increases and Ethereum increases in the same measure, then the correlation would be $r=1$. A correlation of $r=0$ means that the two values have no common properties. For example, the prices of Bitcoin and Ethereum move independently of each other. Causality means that the one value causes the other. This is equivalent to the cause-effect principle: If the pizza is in the oven too long, it will burn. Example: If Bitcoin and Ethereum rise and we know that Ethereum rises because Bitcoin causes it, then we can say that there is causality.

The problem is this: Just because two values show a correlation does not mean that causality is present. So, correlation does not always mean causality. This is called pseudo-correlation. For illustration, the following example: In summer, ice cream turnover and the number of sunburns increase. They correlate. Does this mean that eating ice cream increases the risk of sunburn? Clearly, this is a spurious correlation. On sunny days, the probability of people eating ice cream increases and the probability of getting sunburn increases. Eating ice cream is clearly not the cause of sunburn. On the website "Spurious Correlations" you will find a whole collection of absurd pseudo correlations.

Example: Bitcoin Halving

It is widely accepted that there is a correlation between the Bitcoin Halving and the subsequent positive price breakout of Bitcoin. So far, there have been two Bitcoin Halvings, the first in November 2012 and the second in July 2016, and there has always been a significant increase in the price of Bitcoin after the Halving. The price increase therefore correlates with the halving event. Whether the halving really triggers the increase (causality) has not yet been clearly established. Obviously, chance has its fingers in the pie again. Correlation is therefore not always the same as causality. If correlation is discovered, causality is often suspected where there is none. However, causality is a prerequisite for the correct assessment of a situation.

Example: Google Trends and Bitcoin Price

Visit the Google Trends website and enter "Bitcoin" in the search box. If you compare the search result with the Bitcoin price, you will see that the two curves correlate.

Now the question is: Does Google's search for Bitcoin cause a price increase or do Google searches increase when the Bitcoin price increases? Write down your answer!

It is indeed the case that the rising Bitcoin price increases media attention. The rising number of media reports also increases interest in Bitcoin and Google search queries rise.

Conjunction fallacy: the more accurate the story, the less likely it is

Consider the following examples:

Example 1: What is more likely?
    a) A massive flood disaster, killing more than 1000 people
    b) An earthquake that causes a flood catastrophe in which more than 1000 people die
Write down your answer!

Example 2: What is more likely?
    a) The Bitcoin rate drops from $10,000 to $5,000
    b) Bad news spreads and the Bitcoin price drops from $10,000 to $5,000
Write down your answer!

A fallacy (Latin *fallacia*) is when people do not apply a logical rule that is relevant. The conjunction fallacy is the mistake people make when they judge conjunctions of two events in direct comparison more likely than one of the events. The more detailed an event is described, or the more detailed scenarios are, the more convincing they sound, but the lower their probability becomes. The problem causes a conflict between the logic of probability and the intuition of representativeness. In the examples above, b) sounds more probable because it is the more plausible story. But the probability is lower than in answer a). Example 1 was provided in a study. The probability estimates for the more detailed story b) were higher, although this contradicted the logic. In principle, 89 percent of the people tested in studies on the conjunction fallacy violated the logic of probability. Even in subjects who had attended several lectures on statistics, the percentage was still 85 percent. The story in example 2 that bad news causes the price to fall is more obvious than that the price simply falls. Therefore, in such or similar situations, we commit a conjunction error and believe that the probability of

b) must be greater.

Please also consider the following examples:

Example 3: What is more likely?
  a)   Romeo has hair
  b)   Romeo has blond hair
Write down your answer!

Example 4: What is more likely?
  a)   Julia is a teacher
  b)   Julia is a teacher and cycles to work
Write down your answer!

These two examples have the same logical structure as the previous ones, but they do not produce a false conclusion. The reason is, that the more detailed statement is only more detailed and not more plausible or coherent or a better story. People judge plausibility and coherence instead of asking themselves what the probability behind it would be. Logic prevails when there are no competing, intuitive estimates (as in example 3 and 4). To understand the logic of probabilities, we should think in set diagrams.

Very often in the news we hear or see detailed stories about price rises and falls. The more detailed and plausible a story is, the less likely it is. Paradoxically, however, we are inclined to precisely regard these stories as more probable because they sound more plausible. In addition, correlation-causality errors often occur. For these reasons, you need to be careful when making investment decisions based on the news.

Regression effect: The bad ones will get better

We compare two tennis players. One was exceptionally good

on the first day. This indicates that a good player was lucky. We can assume that he will have a rather good performance on the second day as well, but less successful than on the first day because luck does not last. The second tennis player had an above average bad performance. He was haunted by bad luck. He will have a better performance on the second day, because bad luck probably will not last. The best prediction we can make is that the performance on day two will be mediocre, closer to the average than on day one. Exceptional performances will decrease, bad performances will improve. This is called regression toward the mean, or regression effect. The more extreme the original value is, the more regression we expect, because an extreme value indicates that more luck was involved. This is true if chance has an influence on the measured value and if the two measurements correlate. Correlation and regression are not separate concepts, they are different perspectives on the same concept. The rule is simple: Whenever two measurements do not correlate perfectly, regression to the mean value occurs. This effect is intuitively not easy to understand. We are always looking for a causal explanation and cannot cope with pure statistics. When our attention is drawn to an extraordinary event, our memory searches for the cause. Causal explanations are called up when a regression is detected. However, the explanations are wrong because the regression to the mean has an explanation but no cause.

Consider the following example:
If a stock is better than the market over a year, investors buy that stock because they believe it is superior to the market. If a stock performs worse than the market, investors look for a reason in the weakness of the stock. Often, however, the rise and fall of a share prove to be random fluctuations. The regression to the mean value leads to high values falling again and low values rising again. It has been proven that the purchase of shares that were better than the market over 15 years led to a profit of 95%. The purchase of shares that were

worse than the market led to a profit of 330%. The market itself achieved a profit of 550% over the same period.

Intuitively, people tend to draw conclusions from positive results to positive traits and from negative results to negative traits. However, the principle of regression demands the exact opposite. The more extreme a value is, the more likely it is that the true value is less extreme and closer to the average. Very high values represent an overestimate, very low values represent an underestimate. For average values, errors are equally likely in both directions. Every high value has the potential to sink and every low value has the potential to rise.

If we look at the current Bitcoin chart, we immediately see an extreme value, the all-time high of December 2017 at just under $20,000. This is an extreme value and is probably an overestimate. The regression to the mean value causes the price to approach the mean value again. This is exactly the case, as we can see in the chart.

CHAPTER 7: Principles for successful investing

Why simple rules make us better investors

In clinical predictions, we have known for some time that an algorithm is superior to humans. In 60 percent of the studies, the algorithms proved to be more accurate than humans. The other 40 percent resulted in a draw, but this is a victory for the statistics, as they are much more favorable than the verdict of experts. In the studies it was proven that simple statistical calculations outperform the experts. The reasons why experts are inferior to algorithms are that experts want to be particularly smart, think unconventionally and take complex combinations of features into account in their predictions. Unfortunately, however, complexity generally reduces forecast accuracy. Only in unusual cases does complexity help.

Many studies have shown that human decisions are inferior to a simple prediction formula, even if the result of the formula is communicated to them. This is because they believe they can deliver better results than the formula because they have additional information. But they are usually wrong. A further problem of expert judgements is that humans are unfortunately inconsistent in forming judgements based on complex information. They often give different answers when they judge the same information twice. This is cause for concern because unreliable judgements do not allow valid predictions! Many external and internal influences have an impact on our judgement. Algorithms and formulas do not suffer from this problem. With the same input they always give the same result.

In the following sections we will deal with exactly these simple rules in the form of principles (from lat. *principium* = beginning, origin, principle). They are derived and summarized from the previous chapters. If you follow these principles, you will make rational decisions and avoid unconscious errors of thought. Both will have a positive influence on your investment success.

Make rational decisions

Take a look at the following example:

Decision 1: Choose between:
  a)   A secure profit of $240
  b)   A 25 percent chance of winning $1000 and a 75 percent chance of winning nothing

What do you choose? Write down your answer!

Decision 2: Choose between:
  c)   A safe loss of $750
  d)   A 75 percent chance of losing $1000 and a 25 percent chance of not losing

What do you choose? Write down your answer!

This example provides information about rational decisions. When on the fly, most people feel attracted to a) for decision 1 and d) for decision 2, because we make most quick decisions with our system I. People tend to be risk averse in the area of profits and risk taking in the area of losses. In a survey 73% chose options a) in decision 1 and d) in decision 2, while only 3% preferred the combination b) in decision 1 and c) in decision 2.

Now consider the following example:

ad) A 25 percent chance to win $240 and a 75 percent chance to lose $760.
bc) A 25 percent chance to win $250 and a 75 percent chance to lose $750.

Which of the two options would you choose? Write down your answer!

The choice is easy because option bc) is better than ad). With bc) you win more and lose less than with ad). However, option bc) is exactly the combination from the previous example, which was preferred by only 3% of the respondents, whereas the weaker option ad) was chosen by 73% of the respondents.

As you can see, decision problems can be decomposed or redesigned in such a way that people choose the weaker option. Any choice formulated in terms of "gains" and "losses" can be decomposed in many different ways, so they are likely to produce inconsistent election results. You can also see that it is costly to be risk-averse when you win and risk-averse when you lose. Through these behaviors, people are willing to pay a premium to get a sure win rather than gambling. They are also willing to pay a premium on the expected value to avoid a certain loss. Since both payments come from the same pocket, it is suboptimal if both types of problems occur at the same time. Non-rational people tend to narrow framing because of the WYSIATI rule, they tend to consider only the currently available information and avoid mental effort (non-activation of System II). Therefore, we tend to make decisions to the extent that individual problems arise, even if we are asked to consider them together.

Avoid errors in thinking

Make yourself aware that there are errors in thinking and that we are subject to them. Our brain will do everything it can to prevent you from finding out. Therefore, it is important to keep in mind the errors of thought and the principles derived from them over time so that you can internalize them.

Principles of the two systems

Do not believe your first intuitive answer to a question (System I error). Ask yourself: What do you need to know to give a good answer to a question?

Do not act rashly and without thinking (heuristics). Activate your System II.

Principles of the WYSIATI rule

Be aware that you are subject to the WYSIATI rule when investing and only process the information currently available in the brain.

Activate your System II and search specifically for further and contrary information before you make your judgement.

Be aware that you may become more uncertain in your judgment if you have more information.

Keep a journal. This allows you to recall past situations or events and thus create a more complete history.

Principles on the hindsight bias

The only way to avoid it is to document in detail all factors and the reasons that led to an investment decision. You should therefore write a journal. You write down all news, facts, thoughts and emotions when you make an investment. Since you document everything in detail, you can easily look it up at a later date and thus avoid the hindsight bias.

Principles regarding the outcome bias

As in the case of a return error, you write all the information and emotions that have led to an investment in your journal.

Always evaluate an investment at the time of the decision and not at the end, after you know the result.

Principles regarding the confirmation bias

Question your basic attitude critically. Take the opposite view.

Search for and select specific information that contradicts your basic assumption about what is happening on the market.

Be careful when interpreting the information. Activate your System II to avoid interpreting in the direction of your basic assumptions.

Get feedback from mentors or other investors who take the opposite view.

Principles of clustering illusion

Be aware that we do not recognize what random patterns can look like (see coin flip experiment).

Be aware that our human brain always searches for patterns and also finds them, although there are none.

Do not trust patterns during the technical analysis in the price chart.

Remember that different people ascribe different meanings to different patterns.

Principles of the sunk cost effect

Acquisition costs (i.e., purchase price of a cryptocurrency) are sunk costs and must not be considered when selling. Only the future development potential of the investment counts.

If you have invested a lot of time in technical analysis (such as "Ichimoku Kinko Hyo", Candlestick Patterns etc.) or fundamental analysis but do not get the desired results, you should check to what extent a further investment makes sense.

Principles of the endowment effect

Be aware that the endowment effect exists and that it is more powerful on inexperienced traders.

Be aware that when inexperienced traders buy cryptocurrencies at too high a price, the "unwillingness feeling" increases if the selling price is below the purchase price.

As an experienced trader you must understand cryptocurrencies as a commodity. Ask yourself how much you want to own this cryptocurrency compared to other investments you might have instead.

Principles of optimism bias

If you are in a particularly good mood, you must be especially careful. Your System II is weaker than usual.

Use the ideomotor phenomenon to become more "serious" and therefore not to overestimate it.

If you are generally inclined to be optimistic, be a little more pessimistic in your estimates.

Be a "hyper-realist" and take even small risks seriously.

Compare yourself with the average person to counteract the distortion.

Use past entries in your journal to make more realistic predictions.

Principles of the planning fallacy

Keep in mind that planning fallacy can occur and that schedules and/or costs can be exceeded.

Document. You can use it later for better estimates.

Be more pessimistic about estimates than normal.

Put yourself in a third person's shoes and use the outside view on a problem.

Principles of the anchoring effect

Liquidity in the form of orders (limit, stop loss, take profit, ...) is increasingly accumulating at prominent anchors.

In order not to be subject to the anchoring effect, be aware that you may be influenced by anchors and ask yourself what your answer would look like without anchors.

If you hear statements from friends, experts or gurus, remember that you too are subject to the anchoring effect but do not know the effect.

Principles of priming

Be aware that you are subconsciously primed several times a day and that you yourself subconsciously prime others.

Prime yourself on "success".

Use the ideomotor phenomenon to influence your mood.

Principles of the mere-exposure-effect

You must be aware that this effect exists and that it affects you.

Before investing in cryptocurrencies, you should consider the purchase thoroughly and search for contrary media reports.

Reduce the consumption of news and other media. This reduces the mere-exposure effect.

Keep in mind that just because you know something well or it is generally known, is not necessarily a good investment.

Principles of Framing

Be aware that you react differently depending on how the same information is presented.

Reframe by using as little language as possible and focus on the numerical values.

Always reframe information into a profit frame.
Be aware of unintentional changes in the reference point.

Consider loss trades or loss investments not as losses but as costs. Losses are part of the game. Losses are the stake (=costs).

Think like a securities trader: some win, some lose.

Principles of the halo effect

Do not let the halo effect and social proof from media, experts or gurus mislead you into making an investment decision.

For most results, luck plays a greater role than skill.

Do not rely on other people for your investments.

If you use information from the media, experts or gurus, you must check the information yourself.

Use the "more eyes" principle to evaluate information, decisions or actions of a person.

Principles of illusion of competence

Do not trust experts. Their predictions are usually no better than the result of a coin toss.

However, if you use information or forecasts from third parties for your investment decision, you must activate your System II and check them yourself.

Principles of the insight illusion

Be aware that luck often simply plays a much greater role in good investments.

Note the regression to the mean value.

Do not listen to "recipes for success" from others.

Principles of the overconfidence bias

Make yourself aware that you are subject to hubris.

Question yourself, be skeptical when making predictions for possible investments.

Get feedback from the outside (outside perspective).

Write a journal for your trades and investments, you will see how often you make mistakes. Accept your mistakes, it's part of the game.

Estimate confidence intervals and outliers and write them down in your journal. Try to give better and better estimates and keep the outliers at 20 percent.

Principles of the prospect theory

You must include the reference point.

You should view gains and losses as changes in asset value and not as asset states.

You must be aware that you react emotionally differently to gains and losses and keep this in mind.

Principles of loss aversion

Be aware of the fact of loss aversion. Loss aversion leads to irrational behavior and must be avoided in order to make good investment decisions.

Invest for the long term and do not pay attention to the daily fluctuations.

Consider losses as a necessary evil. When a position is at a loss, see it as a "running" cost to playing in the game. It will seldom happen to you that the position runs in the positive direction immediately after you buy it.

Principles of the disposition effect

Close loser positions if there are no particularly good future prospects for these positions.

Take advantage of the year-round tax advantage by closing loser positions. They reduce the profit and thus the tax burden.

Let winning positions continue to run.

Principles of the certainty and possibility effect

Make yourself aware of the possibility effect and the certainty effect.

If you want to make rational decisions, you should not underweight results that are almost certain.

If you want to make rational decisions, you must not overweight results that are unlikely.

Principles of affect heuristics

Be aware that you subconsciously replace the question "What do I think about it" with the easier question "What feelings does it arouse in me" and make your investment decisions based on this.

Be aware that you are guided by your feelings, mood and emotions and make your investment decisions based on them.

Remember that if you like something, you are more willing to invest in it.

Never make big investment decisions in an emotionally unbalanced state.

Never make big investment decisions when you are in a depressed or overoptimistic mood.

If you have a too good/bad feeling when investing, ask where that feeling comes from.

Principles of regret

Be aware that if by "acting" you got into an unsatisfactory situation, you will regret it more.

Before making an investment decision, go into detail about the expectation of regret and you will feel less regret.

Use a journal so that the error of repentance does not additionally increase your sense of regret.

When making a decision with long-term consequences, you should either be very thorough or completely unconcerned.

Keep in mind that if you make an investment where you are uncertain, the feeling of regret will be greater if you lose.

Disappointment principles

In the case of relatively safe investments (i.e., investments with high chances of winning), you should be aware in advance that despite the high probability, it may not be possible to win and that this will lead to disappointment.

Keep in mind that if you make an investment where you are very secure, the feeling of disappointment will be greater if you lose.

Principles about fear and greed

No risk, no return. If you want returns, you must not be too afraid of losing money.

If something is "too good to be true", question it deeply.

Do not be too greedy with your investments, take profits from time to time.

Principles of the availability cascade

Pay attention to the signs of hypes.

Sell positions in hype phases, buy positions in crash phases.

Beware of too much euphoria, FOMO and FUD.

Do not follow the masses.

Principles of the ego-depletion

For important investment decisions, make the decision in the morning and not in the evening.

Avoid important investment decisions after major physical, cognitive or emotional exertion.

Make sure you get sufficient and good quality sleep.

Do not day trade.

Principles to the basic rate fallacy

Consider statistical facts and include them in your decision making.

You should also look at the importance of the probability of the non-occurring event (e.g., what is the probability that it will not rain? What is the loss probability of your trading system?).

If you consider probabilities of an event, you should also consider the probability of the non-event.

The probability of the event and the non-event (counter probability) must always be 100 percent.

Principles of the availability error

Be aware of the availability error.

If you are overly optimistic about something, you must consider whether the availability error is to blame.

Use your journal to minimize the availability error by

reviewing and recalling past investments and trades.

Make decisions based on factual data, not opinions.

Avoid media coverage. The journalists' choice of topics influences the availability error.

Principles of representativeness heuristics

Do not overestimate probabilities just because individual pieces of information have a stronger influence on your judgement.

Be aware that the mean value for higher samples approaches the expected value.

Be aware that the mean value can deviate from the expected value for small samples.

Principles of denominator effect

Note that when you give relative frequencies ("How many", e.g., 1 in 100,000 children), you tend to overestimate.

In order to gain a better understanding of numbers and to put the emotional impact of information into perspective, you should convert information about opportunities, risks or probabilities ("How likely") and relative frequencies ("How many") into each other and then compare them.

Principles of the correlation-causality error

Note that correlation does not mean causality.

Look for cause-and-effect mechanisms.

Do not be fooled by spurious correlations.

Principles of the conjunction fallacy

Keep in mind that in a direct comparison you consider the linkage of two events more likely than one of the events.

Be aware that the more accurate (or detailed) a story is, the less likely it is.

Principles of the regression effect

Be aware that the regression effect exists, although it is not intuitively understandable.

Remember that the more an extreme value deviates from the mean value, the more likely it is to regress back to the mean value.

Do not trust experts

As you have learned in the previous chapters, you should not trust experts. When can we even trust expert judgements?
There are two basic requirements for the acquisition of expertise:

1. an environment that is regular in order to be predictable and
2. the possibility to learn these regularities through years of practice

Only if these two conditions are met, intuitive predictions can probably be correct. This applies for example to chess, bridge, poker, doctors, nurses, firefighters, etc. Gaining expertise also depends on the speed and quality of the feedback you receive about your judgments. So, the rule is: if there are no stable regularities in the environment, one cannot trust intuition. Examples of this are stock pickers and political scientists. They operate in an environment in which information has no validity for forecasts (zero validity environment). Their proven failure confirms the fundamental unpredictability of the events they try to predict.

In environments with less regularity and low predictability, they use judgment heuristics. Often System I tricks us and replaces a difficult question with an easier one to find a quick answer. This answer can be plausible enough to pass the loose test of System II and we don't question it.

Conclusion: crypto-markets are environments where there are no stable regularities, which is why experts cannot make correct long-term predictions. Therefore, do not rely on experts and better create your own investment rules that you adhere to and that you constantly develop.

Control your emotions

In order to control our emotions, we need to internalize the mindset of professional traders to bring ourselves closer to rational behavior. The way of thinking is:

"Some investments we win and some we lose!"

The main purpose of this mantra is to control the emotions when you lose. Because losses are much more painful emotionally (on average 2.5 times) than gains are gratifying. A wide framing reduces the loss aversion, because it is one of many decisions. The combination of narrow framing and loss aversion (e.g., I have to sell every single position with profit) is very expensive. With wide framing you can avoid this trap, take advantage of the emotional benefits and save time, money and hassle by reducing the frequency of having to look at how your investments are performing. Short-term tracking of value fluctuations is a losing proposition, because the annoyance of frequent small losses outshines the joy of equally frequent gains. Targeted ignoring of short-term results improves the quality of results and investment decisions on the one hand and the emotional quality of life on the other.

The typical short-term reaction to bad news and falling prices is an increased loss aversion. Investors who receive summary feedback less frequently, see bad news or short price declines much less frequently, are probably less risk averse and are more likely to build up higher assets in the long term. They are also less susceptible to constant, costly portfolio shifts if they do not know how individual positions will perform in the short term. The effort not to change the securities positions over several periods is rewarded with better performance.

Keep a journal

Keep a journal (diary) for your investments or trades. Write down everything that was relevant for the investment decisions or the trades. Additionally, write down your feelings, moods and emotions.

The advantages of a journal are:
- Avoidance of hindsight bias by not mistakenly remembering wrong facts that were made at the time of the investment.
- Minimizing the availability error by recalling past investments or trades, setups, information and errors.
- Avoiding the outcome bias by not judging the investment by the result, but by the quality of the decision at the time of the decision.
- Avoidance of the WYSIATI rule, by remembering things that are not present in our head at the moment.
- Minimizing the distortion of optimism by analyzing past investments and thus providing more realistic estimates.
- Minimizing overestimation of our own abilities, by seeing that we always make mistakes in our decisions.
- Identifying bad decisions because we let our emotions guide us.
- Avoiding remorse by writing about the feeling of regret in the journal.
- Managing emotions like fear and greed.
- Seeing when your ability to make good decisions is exhausted (ego depletion) by recording when you trade or invest and when you are physically, mentally or physically active.
- Identify recurring patterns or errors in investing.
- Perform simple statistical calculations such as percentage of winners, percentage of losers, average

profits, average losses, expected values, maximum profit, maximum loss, etc.

- To be able to test trading or investment strategies.
- Estimate future prices and confidence intervals.
- To identify outliers.
- To see how good your own forecast accuracy is.
- And much more.

Writing a journal means additional work in the beginning, but as you can see from the list above, the advantages outweigh the disadvantages by far. To make rational and therefore good investment decisions, you should keep a journal.

Calculate expected values

The expected value is a term from stochastics. The expected value of a random variable describes the number, which the random variable assumes on average.

$$EV = Pw * G - Pl * V$$

EV ... Expected value
Pw ... Probability of winning
G ... Amount of profit
Pl ... Probability of loss
V ... Amount of the loss

The expected value is thus calculated from the product of the probability of winning with the gains minus the product of the probability of losing with the losses. The expected value is positive if the first term is greater than the second.

Look again at the example from the beginning of this chapter:

Decision 1: Choose between:
   a)   A safe profit of $240
   b)   A 25 percent chance to win $1000 and a 75 percent chance to win nothing

Decision 2: Choose between:
   c)   A safe loss of $750
   d)   A 75 percent chance of losing $1000 and a 25 percent chance of losing nothing

The expected value at decision 1b) is calculated as follows:
$$EV = 0{,}25 * 1000 - 0{,}75 * 0 = 250$$

The expected value at decision 2b) is calculated as follows:
$$EV = 0{,}25 * 0 - 0{,}75 * 1000 = -750$$

Now look at the further specification:

ad) A 25 percent chance of winning $240 and a 75 percent chance of losing $760.

bc) A 25 percent chance to win $250 and a 75 percent chance to lose $750.

The expected value at decision ad) is calculated as follows:
$$EV = 0{,}25 * 240 - 0{,}75 * 760 = -510$$

The expected value at decision bc) is calculated as follows
$$EV = 0{,}25 * 250 - 0{,}75 * 750 = -500$$

By calculating the expected values, you can easily see how you should have decided when you look at the situation from a rational point of view. Namely for answer b) in decision 1 and for answer c) in decision 2.

Let's look at the competition of framing from chapter 2 and calculate the expected values. The first question was: *Would you enter a lottery with a 10 percent chance of winning $95 and a 90 percent chance of losing $5?*

The expected value is calculated as follows:
$$EV = 0.1 * 95 - 0.9 * 5 = 5$$

The second question was: *Would you pay $5 to enter a contest that has a 10 percent chance of winning $100 and a 90 percent chance of winning nothing?*

The expected value is calculated as follows:
$$EV = 0{,}1 * 100 - 0{,}9 * 0 = 10 - 5 = 5$$

The expected value in the second question is $10. But since you have to pay $5 to play the lottery, we have to deduct this from the expected value and get $5 as a result. So, you see that the expected values of the two questions are identical and would rationally decide the same for both questions. As you have seen in the chapter Framing, this would not be the case if one were to decide based on the question alone. So, we can avoid irrational decisions caused by framing by calculating the expected value.

Let's look at the examples from chapter 4, Prospect theory:

Example 1: What do you choose?
   a)   *Receive $900 safely or*
   b)   *a 90 percent chance to win $1000?*

Example 2: What do you choose?
   a)   *A safe loss of $900 or*
   b)   *a 90 percent probability of losing $1000?*

The expected value for example 1 and 2 for answer b) is: 0.9*1000=900 USD. It is therefore identical with the value in example 1 and 2 a).

Example 3: In addition to your current assets, you will receive $1000. Decide on one of the following options:
   a)   *A 50 percent chance to win $1000 or*
   b)   *$500 safely received*

Example 4: In addition to your current assets, you will receive $2000. Decide on one of the following options:
   a)   *A 50 percent chance of losing $1000 or*
   b)   *$500 safe to lose*

In example 3 and 4, the expected value for option a) is 0.5*1000=500 USD and thus identical to option b).

The expected values of the choices in the examples are always identical. The difference is that it is "certain" in one case and "probable" in the other. This leads to the fact that we do not act rationally.

Consider the coin toss example from Chapter 4, Loss Aversion:

We flip a coin once. If you toss a number, you lose $100. Heads, you win $150. Would you take this gamble?

The expected value in this example is calculated:
$$EV = 0,5 * 150 - 0,5 * 100 = 25$$

The probability of winning or losing a fair coin toss is 50% each. The expected value is therefore $25. From a rational point of view, you would always have to make such bets.

Let's also look at the problems with the Allais paradox from chapter 4:

Problem A: Choose between
1. *A 61 percent chance to win $520,000 or*
2. *A 63 percent chance to win $500,000*

The expected values are calculated as follows:
$$EV = 0,61 * 520.000 = 317.200$$
$$EV = 0,63 * 500.000 = 315.000$$

Problem B: Choose between
1. *A 98 percent chance of winning $520,000 or*
2. *A 100 percent chance to win $500,000*

The expected values are calculated as follows:
$$EV = 0,98 * 520.000 = 509.600$$
$$EV = 1,00 * 500.000 = 500.000$$

If you follow the rules of rationality, you would have to choose answer 1 for problem A and B, because it has the higher expected value.

Expected value of your investments

You should calculate the expected value for your investments (or your investment strategy) when you log your hit rate and loss rate as well as profits and losses. See the following example:

Of every ten investments or trades made, three are winners and seven are losers. This means that your hit rate is 30 percent, and your loss rate is 70 percent. If your profits are now the same size as your losses, for example $100, this results in an expected value of:

$$EV = 0,3 * 100 - 0,7 * 100 = -40$$

So, on average you lose $40 with every investment.

However, if your profits are three times as large ($300) as the losses, the expected value is as follows:

$$EV = 0,3 * 300 - 0,7 * 100 = 20$$

Although the hit rate is only 30 percent, this results in a positive expected value of $20. This means that a system that loses more often than it wins can still make a profit if the gains are greater than the losses. So, to establish a positive investment balance, you need to either

    a)   Increase the probability of winning (or decrease the probability of losing) or

    b)   increase profits (or decrease losses).

Establish the Bayesian way of thinking

The Bayesian way of thinking comes from the mathematician Thomas Bayes. He also developed Bayes' theorem, which is of great importance in probability theory. He coined the term "Bayesian probability", named after him, which interprets probability as a degree of personal conviction. It differs from objectivist concepts of probability, which interpret probabilities as relative frequencies.

There are two things we should remember: First, without having any further information about a subject, base rates are important (see base rate fallacy). This is often not intuitively obvious. Secondly, our intuitive impressions about the significance of the available information are often exaggerated. As described above, we tend to believe the stories we make up ourselves.

For a statistically correct evaluation (without having to master statistics) we remember two rules for Bayesian thinking:
1. anchor your judgement about the probability of a result in a plausible base rate
2. question the significance of the information

If no new useful information is available (or the quality of the information is poor), the Bayesian solution is to stick to the base rate.

Use the pre-mortem method

The pre-mortem method is a simple and quick method to find yet unknown risks and to avoid some distortions, such as optimism bias, planning mistakes and overestimation of oneself.

With the pre-mortem method, we imagine that we are, for example, one year into the future. An investment according to today's plan was implemented, but the result is unfortunately an absolute disaster. Now we take 10 to 20 minutes to write a short story about this catastrophe. Which reasons and circumstances led to this disaster? The important thing about this method is that it leaves room for doubt and you can look for dangers that you hadn't thought of before. It is not a panacea, but it does limit the potential damage of plans, estimates or predictions that are subject to the distortions of information availability, the WYSIATI rule and excessive optimism. If you find other risks, include them in your assessment and make a correction.

Use hypothesis testing

The hypothesis test is a method from statistics with which one wants to prove a claim with collected data. The principle of these statistical tests is that the opposite must be disproved. There are two assertions/conjectures, the so-called hypotheses, which are opposed to each other. The null hypothesis to be tested and its opposite, the alternative or counterhypothesis. If the counterhypothesis can be proved, then the basic assumption, the null hypothesis, has to be rejected.

For our application purposes we will not perform statistical calculations. It is basically a matter of taking the other side's point of view in order to be able to make better investment decisions and to eliminate or at least minimize errors of thought, such as optimism bias, overestimation of one's own abilities, availability errors, WYSIATI rule, etc.

For illustration purposes, consider the following example:
Imagine that your default setting is that Bitcoin will increase. So, this is the null hypothesis. The counterhypothesis is therefore that Bitcoin will fall. We now must search for facts to prove the counterhypothesis. If we succeed in doing so, we must reject the basic assumption (that Bitcoin will rise). You may not be able to prove or disprove both hypotheses one hundred percent. But by working intensively on the counterhypothesis to refute the null-hypothesis, you will have a more comprehensive picture of a situation (such as current market developments) and thus be able to make better investment decisions.

Behavior in case of crash and hype

How should investors react to hype and crash? John D. Rockefeller, an American entrepreneur and the first billionaire in world history, is believed to have said

> "The way to make money is to buy,
> when blood is running in the streets."

This means if the stock markets are writing massive losses, it is time to buy. So, we act against the current. When everyone is panicking, not thinking rationally, guided by their emotions and selling quickly, we stay calm and buy cheap. So, a stock market crash offers a good buying opportunity. When all the media are calling for selling, then it is a good time to buy. But only if the future prospects of the investment are really positive.

The opposite is when we are in a phase of hypes, boom or bubble. Warren Buffet, a major US investor and entrepreneur, is believed to have said

> "Be Fearful When Others Are Greedy and
> Greedy When Others Are Fearful."

This means that when we are in a crash phase and everyone is anxious, we should be greedy and grab. In the case of a hype, when all others are greedy and the price is always reaching new heights, we should be greedy and take positions.

People enter the market much too late at high prices just to make some money quickly. The consequence is that in most cases losses due to falling prices, are the result of the hype. Thus, it happened also with the Bitcoin Hype in December 2017 as people, influenced by the hype and overvalued bitcoin price, entered and bought at an inflated price. The disillusionment followed after the price turned around at approx. $20,000 and collapsed to almost $3000 within one year. When prices rise, new profits are made every day and new highs are reached, we quickly forget that everything that rises can also fall again. Examples of this are:

- Black Monday, October 1987
- Japan crisis, 1990
- Dotcom bubble, March 2000
- Terrorist attacks on the World Trade Center, September 11, 2001
- Global financial crisis, 2007
- Bitcoin and Altcoin bubble, early 2018
- Coronavirus crisis, March 2020

The hype is the last phase of the bubble before it bursts. The only problem is that we usually do not realize that it was a bubble until it's too late.

There are many more opportunities on the market that will come in the future. The bad thing is to always chase a missed opportunity and therefore make a bad decision. Benjamin Graham, author of the book "The Intelligent Investor" and mentor of Warren Buffet is believed to have said

"Patience is the first virtue of the investor"

Have patience, the next investment opportunity will surely come.

Closing words

Successful investing does not require high intelligence. Most are simply lucky. For those of us who have not been lucky is important: to have a reflective mind, be rational and do not be lazy in thinking (activation of System II). Many mistakes in investing happen because we rely on our intuitive actions without questioning them. Another weakness of people is that it is easier and more pleasant to recognize and name the mistakes of others than our own. Even under favorable circumstances, we find it difficult to question our beliefs and principles, and we find it especially difficult when it is most necessary. We can benefit from a factually sound and objective opinion of others. Our mistakes have characteristic patterns that we ourselves usually do not recognize. Systematic errors of thought (distortions, heuristics) occur in a predictable way under certain circumstances. We are convinced of the correctness of our decisions and judgements even when we are wrong. An objective observer, a mentor, recognizes the errors with a higher probability than we can. Look for a mentor! A person who will pass on his or her professional and experiential knowledge to you. This will save you a lot of time, money and mental stress.

Especially in the crypto-world there is a lot of ignorance and unfortunately, also a lot of fraud. Therefore, I would like to give you the following principle as final advice:

Rely on facts, not on opinions!

Acknowledgement

Thank you, dear reader, for purchasing this book. I hope I was able to open your eyes and provide added value.

The basis for my success as an author in self-publishing are recommendations on Amazon. Therefore, I ask you for two minutes of your valuable time to give the book an evaluation. You can also rate if you did not buy the book yourself.

Go to amazon's web page and search for: "Wolfgang Fallmann" or "Crypto Investor Mindset". Click on the book, scroll all the way down to "Review this product" and click on "Write a customer review". Describe briefly what you liked or what helped you most. Thanks a lot!

I am at your disposal for further questions, wishes, suggestions or criticism. Please contact me at: info@wolfgangfallmann.com or visit my website: www.btc-machine.com

I look forward to hearing from you!

About the author

Wolfgang Fallmann, born 1982 in Austria, studied mechanical engineering at the Technical University of Vienna and technical management at the FH Campus Wien. He developed automated currency trading systems (so-called Forex Robots) and was a Forex day trader. In 2014 he came into contact with cryptocurrencies. Wolfgang developed one of the first Bitcoin ATMs in Austria and participated in the development of the Monero Hardware Wallet. Later he founded a mining company to mine cryptocurrencies. He operated staking and financed master nodes. Wolfgang invests in stocks, ETFs, P2P loans, Bitcoin, Bitcoin Futures & Options and other cryptocurrencies. He passes on his decades of accumulated knowledge about investments, block chain and cryptocurrencies in lectures, workshops and books. He is the founder of "Bitcoin Machine" (www.btc-machine.com), editor of the regularly published "Bitcoin Machine Insight Reports" and author of the book "Bitcoin COT Bible", the first book on the use of the Commitment of Traders Report for Bitcoin Investments.

Glossary

Affect Heuristic
Affect heuristics means that we consult our mood, feelings and emotions when making judgements and decisions

All Time High (ATH)
The highest price ever reached.

All Time Low (ATL)
The lowest price ever reached.

Altcoins
Altcoins are all cryptocurrencies that are not Bitcoin.

Anchoring Effect
The anchoring effect, also known as anchor heuristics, is the fact that people are influenced in their number estimations by existing environmental information (especially by numbers) without being aware of this influence.

Availability Error
The availability error, also called availability heuristic, is the tendency to overestimate the probability of events with higher "availability" in memory.

Availability Cascade
The availability cascade is a self-sustaining chain of events, triggered by media reports about a mostly insignificant event.

Base Rate Fallacy
To put it simply, the base rate fallacy is the neglect of statistical facts.

Black Swan
A Black Swan is a metaphor for an unforeseen, sudden risk that leads to a massive price collapse and investors lose their money.

Certainty Effect
In the certainty effect, events that are almost certain are underweighted in relation to their probability.

Clustering illusion
The clustering illusion is the tendency to recognize random patterns in sufficiently large (random) amounts of data and to ascribe meaning to them.

Coins
Cryptocurrencies are also called "coins".

Confirmation Bias
The confirmation bias is the tendency of people to seek, select and interpret information in such a way that it confirms their own expectations.

Conjunction fallacy
The conjunction fallacy is the mistake that people make when they are more likely to judge the conjunction of two outcomes in direct comparison than one of the outcomes.

Correlation-causality error
The correlation-causality error (also fallacy from correlation to causality, Latin *Cum hoc ergo propter hoc*) happens when one confuses pure correlation with causality.

Cost Averaging
"Cost averaging" or "cost average effect" is the fact that an investor can buy more units for the same amount when prices are falling and fewer units when prices are rising, thus buying or selling at an average price.

Denominator Effect

Denominator effect means that events with a low probability are weighted much more heavily when they are described in categories of relative frequencies ("How many", e.g., 1 in 100,000 children) than when they are expressed in abstract terms such as opportunities, risks or probabilities ("How likely", e.g., 0.001%).

Disposition Effect

The disposition effect is the tendency of investors to sell the positions that have increased in value and to hold the positions that have decreased in value.

Ego-Depletion

The ego-depletion (from Latin *ego* 'I' and neo-Latin *depletio* 'bloodletting', to deplore 'emptying'; here in the sense of "self-exhaustion") is the self-exhaustion by physical, cognitive or emotional effort.

Endowment Effect

The endowment effect is the phenomenon that for people the value of a good increases when they own it.

Fallacy

A fallacy (from Latin *fallacia*) is when people do not apply a logical rule that is relevant.

Framing

Framing is the tendency to draw different conclusions when the same information is presented differently.

Halo-Effect

The halo effect is a distortion in which one concludes from known characteristics of a person to unknown characteristics.

Heuristic

A heuristic is a "mental shortcut" of thinking.

Hindsight bias
The hindsight bias is also called the "I knew it all along" effect. It is the tendency of people to believe in retrospect that they knew something that they could prove but did not know.

Hodler
A crypto-investor who constantly buys cryptocurrencies and holds them for a very long time, since they hope for massive price growth.

Ideomotor phenomenon
The ideomotor phenomenon, also known as the Carpenter effect, influences an action through a performance. This means that the seeing or thinking of a certain movement triggers the tendency to perform that very movement.

Illusion of competence
The competence illusion is the mistaken belief that competent people can make better predictions.

Insight illusion
Insight illusions arise because we tend to reverse causal relationships due to the halo effect.

Limit Order
A limit order is an order to buy or sell a certain number of crypto currencies at a fixed or better price.

Loss Aversion
The aversion to loss is the aversion of people to loss.

Market Order
A market order is an order to buy or sell a cryptocurrency from a broker at the best current market price.

Mere-Exposure-Effect
The mere-exposure effect is the fact that people develop a

more positive attitude towards images, videos or words that are shown more often.

Mining
Mining is the process by which new cryptocurrencies are created by using computing power.

Optimism Bias
Optimism bias or optimistic bias is a cognitive bias that makes people believe that they are more likely to experience a positive event themselves.

Outcome bias
Outcome bias is the tendency of people to judge a decision by its end result rather than by the quality of the decision at the time of the decision.

Overconfidence Bias
Overconfidence bias or overconfidence effect is a form of systematic misjudgment of one's own abilities, knowledge and skills.

Planning Fallacy
The planning fallacy is the tendency of people and companies to underestimate the time (and cost) it takes to complete a task or project.

Possibility Effect
The possibility effect overweights unlikely events disproportionately.

Priming
Priming is the tendency for a stimulus, such as a word, image, smell, gesture or similar, to unconsciously activate memory content and thus influence our decisions.

Prospect Theory

The prospect theory forms the basis of behavioral economics and examines decision making under risk.

Pump & Dump
Pump & dump refers to a form of market manipulation (or fraud) in which the price is artificially increased ("pumped up") by false and misleading positive statements or by massive purchases in order to sell the previously cheaply purchased stock at a higher price to bona fide investors. As soon as the operators of the system sell their overvalued cryptocurrencies (English *dump* for 'get rid of'), the price sinks and the bona fide investors lose their money.

Regression Effect
The regression effect, or regression toward the mean, is the phenomenon that, after an extremely unusual measurement value, the following one is closer to the average again. This is the case when chance has an influence on the measured value and when the two measurements correlate.

Representativeness Heuristic
Representativeness heuristic is a bias in which decision makers estimate the probability of occurrence of events to be higher if they better represent the underlying population.

Resistance
A resistance is a horizontal line above the current price generated by several highs at the same level. It is an obstacle for the price because it is difficult to break through to the top.

Stock Picker
A stock picker is an investor who tries to achieve an above-average return by specifically investing in individual stocks.

Stop Loss
A stop loss (SL) order is a limit order to limit risk.

Sunk-Cost-Effect
The sunk cost effect is the tendency to stick with a project for a longer period of time if an investment in the form of time, effort or money has already been made.

Support
A support is a horizontal line below the current price generated by several lows at the same level. It is a support for the price as it is difficult to break through to the bottom.

Take Profit
A take profit (TP) order is a limit order to take a profit.

WYSIATI-Rule
The WYSIATI rule stands for "What you see is all there is". Our brain only processes the information that is currently available.

Sources

Below is a list of sources that have influenced this book.

Books

Predictably Irrational, Revised and Expanded Edition: The Hidden Forces That Shape Our Decisions – Dan Ariely, 2010. ISBN: 978-0061353246

The Honest Truth About Dishonesty: How We Lie to Everyone--Especially Ourselves – Dan Ariely, 2013. ISBN: 978-0062183613

The Upside of Irrationality: The Unexpected Benefits of Defying Logic – Dan Ariely, 2011. ISBN: 978-0061995040

The Halo Effect: . . . and the Eight Other Business Delusions That Deceive Managers - Phil Rosenzweig, 2014. ISBN: 978-1476784038

The Black Swan: The Impact of the Highly Improbable - Nassim Nicholas Taleb, 2010. ISBN: 978-0812973815

Skin in the Game: Hidden Asymmetries in Daily Life - Nassim Nicholas Taleb, 2018. ISBN: 978-3328600268

Fooled by Randomness: The Hidden Role of Chance in Life and in the Markets - Nassim Nicholas Taleb, 2007. ISBN: 978-0141031484

Built to Last: Successful Habits of Visionary Companies - Jim Collins & Jerry I. Porras, 2003. ISBN: 978-3421056504

The Intelligent Investor - Benjamin Graham, 2006. ISBN: 978-0060555665

Principles: Life and Work - Ray Dalio, 2017. ISBN: 978-1501124020

Thinking, Fast and Slow - Daniel Kahneman, 2013. ISBN: 978-0374533557

Influence: The Psychology of Persuasion - Robert B. Cialdini, 2006. ISBN: 978-0061241895

Checklist Manifesto – Atul Gawande, 2011. ISBN: 978-0312430009

John Sutton: Sunk Costs and Market Structure: Price Competition, Advertising, and the Evolution of Concentration. Mcgraw Hill Book Co; Auflage: 1st MIT Press Pbk. Ed (30. September 2007). ISBN 978-0262693585

David Aronson: Evidence-Based Technical Analysis: Applying the Scientific Method and Statistical Inference to Trading Signals. In: Band 274 von Wiley Trading. John Wiley & Sons, 2011. ISBN 978-1-118-16058-9. Kapitel 2: The intuitive judgment and the role of heuristics.

Papers

Representativeness (Subjective Probability: A Judgment of Representativeness. Cognitive Psychology 3, 1972, 430-454)

Young, A. (2011). Prospect Theory: An Analysis of Decision Under Risk (Kahneman and Tversky, 1979).

Tversky, A., & Kahneman, D. (1974). Judgment under Uncertainty: Heuristics and Biases. Science, 185 4157, 1124-31 .

Kahneman, D., & Tversky, A. (1979). Prospect theory: An analysis of decision under risk Econometrica 47.

Tversky, A., & Kahneman, D. (1981). The framing of decisions and the psychology of choice. Science, 211 4481, 453-8 .

Kahneman, D. (2003). A perspective on judgment and choice: mapping bounded rationality. The American psychologist, 58 9, 697-720.

Kahneman, D., & Tversky, A. (1984). Choices, values, and frames.

Tversky, A., & Kahneman, D. (1991). Loss Aversion in Riskless Choice: A Reference-Dependent Model.

Kahneman, D. (2003). Maps of Bounded Rationality: Psychology for Behavioral Economics.

Kahneman, D., & Tversky, A. (1973). On the Psychology of Prediction.

Kahneman, D., Knetsch, J.L., & Thaler, R.H. (1990). Experimental tests of the endowment effect and the coase theorem

Kahneman, D., & Frederick, S. (2002). Representativeness revisited: Attribute substitution in intuitive judgment.

Kahneman, D., & Lovallo, D. (1993). Timid Choices and Bold Forecasts: A Cognitive Perspective on Risk Taking.

Kahneman, D. (2003). Maps of bounded rationality: A perspective on intuitive judgment and choice.

Kahneman, D., & Tversky, A. (1996). On the reality of cognitive illusions. Psychological review, 103 3, 582-91; discussion 592-6.

Tversky, A., & Kahneman, D. (1971). Belief in the law of small numbers.

Kahneman, D. (2003). A Psychological Perspective on Economics.

P. Slovic, M. L. Finucane, E. Peters, D. G. MacGregor: The affect heuristic. In: T. Gilovich, D. Griffin, D. Kahneman (Hrsg.): Heuristics and biases: The psychology of intuitive judgment. Cambridge University Press, New York 2002, S. 397–420.

Amos Tversky, Daniel Kahneman: Judgment under Uncertainty: Heuristics and Biases. In: Science. Band 185, Nr. 4157, 27. September 1974

A. Tversky, D. Kahneman: Availability: A heuristic for judging frequency and probability. In: Cognitive Psychology. Band 42, 1973, S. 207–232

Jack L. Knetsch: The Endowment Effect and Evidence of Nonreversible Indifference Curves. In: The American Economic Review. Bd. 79, Nr. 5, December 1989, S. 1277–1284.

Peter Wason: Reasoning about a rule. In: Quarterly Journal of Experimental Psychology, Band 20, 1968, ISSN 0033-555X, S. 273–281.

Hersh Shefrin, Meir Statman: The Disposition to Sell Winners Too Early and Ride Losers Too Long: Theory and Evidence. In: The Journal of Finance, 40. Jg. Nr. 3, doi:10.2307/2327802, S. 777–790 (English).

R. F. Baumeister, E. Bratslavsky, M. Muraven, D. M. Tice: Ego depletion: Is the active self a limited resource? In: Journal of Personality and Social Psychology. 74, 1998, S. 1252–1265.

Gino, Francesca; Moore, Don A.; Bazerman, Max H. (2009). "No Harm, No Foul: The Outcome Bias in Ethical

Judgments" (PDF). SSRN 1099464. Harvard Business School Working Paper, No. 08-080.

D. Kahneman, A. Tversky (Hrsg.): Choices, values and frames. Cambridge University Press, Cambridge 2000.

William B. Carpenter: Essays Scientific and philosophical, D. Appelton and Company 1889, S. 182 ff

Moreland & Zajonc (1982): Exposure effects in person perception: Familiarity, similarity, and attraction. Journal of Experimental Social Psychology, 18, S. 395–415

O'Sullivan, Owen P. (2015). The neural basis of always looking on the bright side. Dialogues in Philosophy, Mental and Neuro Sciences, 8(1):11–15.

Stephen Palmer: The effects of contextual scenes on the identification of objects. In: Memory and Cognition. Nr. 3, 1975, S. 519–526.

Murphy, Sheila & Zajonc, Robert. (1993). Affect, Cognition, and Awareness: Affective Priming with Optimal and Suboptimal Stimulus Exposures. Journal of personality and social psychology. 64. 723-39. 10.1037//0022-3514.64.5.723.

Stigler, Stephen M (1997). "Regression toward the mean, historically considered". Statistical Methods in Medical Research. 6 (2): 103–114.

B. Fischhoff: Hindsight ≠ foresight: the effect of outcome knowledge on judgment under uncertainty. In: Journal of Experimental Psychology: Human Perception and Performance. Band 1, Nr. 3, 1975, S. 288–299

Baruch Fischhoff, Ruth Beyth: "I knew it would happen". Remembered Probabilities of Once-Future Things. In:

Organizational Behavior and Human Performance. Band 13, Nr. 1, 1975, S. 1–16

Don A. Moore, Deborah A. Small: Error and Bias in Comparative Judgment: On Being Both Better and Worse Than We Think We Are. Journal of Personality and Social Psychology, 2007, Vol. 92, No. 6, 972–989.

Barber, Brad M. and Odean, Terrance, Trading is Hazardous to Your Wealth: The Common Stock Investment Performance of Individual Investors.

Links

https://www.tylervigen.com/spurious-correlations

The Invisible Gorilla: And Other Ways Our Intuitions Deceive Us: www.theinvisiblegorilla.com

The Monkey Business Illusion:
https://www.youtube.com/watch?v=IGQmdoK_ZfY

Index

https://btc-machine.com

Bitcoin Report
Tools
Mentoring
and more

Imprint
Wolfgang Fallmann
Oberdörfl 25, 9072 Ludmannsdorf
Austria, Europe
info@wolfgangfallmann.com

Made in the USA
Las Vegas, NV
14 February 2021

17758300R00090